The Family Cabin

The Family Cabin

Inspiration for Camps, Cottages, and Cabins

DALE MULFINGER, author of *The Cabin* and *Back to the Cabin*

The Taunton Press

The Taunton Press
Inspiration for hands-on living®

The Taunton Press, Inc.
63 South Main Street
PO Box 5506
Newtown, CT 06470-5506
e-mail: tp@taunton.com

EDITOR: Peter Chapman
COPY EDITOR: Diane Sinitsky
ART DIRECTOR: Rosalind Loeb
JACKET/COVER DESIGN: Alison Wilkes
INTERIOR DESIGN: Alison Wilkes
LAYOUT: Alison Wilkes
ILLUSTRATOR: Christine Erikson

The following names/manufacturers appearing in *The Family Cabin* are trademarks:
Airstream®, Benjamin Moore®, Cor-ten®, Energy Star®, Formica®, Jiffy Lube®,
Kynar®, Lincoln Logs®, Monopoly®, Parallam®, PolyWhey®, Thermomass®, Yahtzee®

Library of Congress Cataloging-in-Publication Data
Names: Mulfinger, Dale, 1943- author.
Title: The family cabin : inspiration for camps, cottages, and cabins /
Dale Mulfinger.
Description: Newtown, CT : The Taunton Press, Inc., 2017.
Identifiers: LCCN 2017007155 | ISBN 9781631866524 (hardcover)
ISBN 9781631866586 (paperback)
Subjects: LCSH: Vacation homes--United States. | Cottages--United States. |
  Log cabins--United States.
Classification: LCC NA7575 .M847 2017 | DDC 728.7/20973--dc23
LC record available at https://lccn.loc.gov/2017007155

PRINTED IN CHINA
10 9 8 7 6 5 4 3 2 1

Dedication

To the many current and future cabin owners who continue to present me with such rich material for stories, ideas, and photos.

Of special note is my brief friendship with the late cabin owner Jake Franssen. May he enjoy Rome from a new and better view.

Acknowledgments

I'm grateful for the unending help from my wife, Jan; the editing by Peter Chapman; the artful eye of Rosalind Loeb; and the exceptional photography of Susan Teare, Troy Thies, Carolyn Bates, and others.

Contents

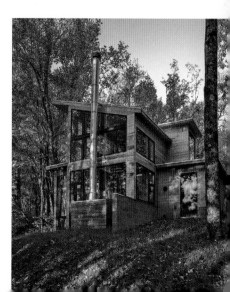

LIKE MANY OTHER cabin owners, I have an extended "family" that enjoys our cabin. There's my wife, two daughters, their husbands, and our four grandchildren. Then there are our

Introduction

(unrelated) cabin co-owners, who have no children or grandchildren of their own but lots of family and friends to share cabin life with. So for us, and for many cabin dwellers, "the family cabin" has a broad and varied definition beyond our immediate relatives.

Regardless of exactly who lives there, cabins at their most basic level are places of human bonding, where family and friends relinquish privacy in favor of familial intimacy and creating a legacy of stories and lore. Cabins are where Grandpa scores the growth of grandchildren by way of notches on the kitchen door-frame. This is where Uncle Bob's big bass catch graces the dining area and Aunt Mary's knitted afghan drapes the back of the couch.

Cabins line the shores of our lakes and rivers and nestle under tall pines, just waiting for our families to come together. Young and old gather around fire pits, where sing-alongs and s'mores enrich a starry gathering

Cabins, first and foremost, are about a great place to escape to.

of family revelry. Docks, decks, and porches enhance life in the great outdoors where fishing, dining, and sleeping are fresh-air rituals.

Families have been taking respite from the grind of urban life since the beginning of the 20th century, gathering together in cabins great and small to recharge their batteries in the realm of nature. Retreating into the fresh air of the country from the smog-filled cities was initiated as a preventive health measure. Mothers and children went away for the summer and Dad would escape to join them as often as he could. Life at the family cabin included planting a vegetable garden, raising farm animals for eggs and milk, and foraging in the wild for berries, mushrooms, and other morsels.

Some family cabins, camps, and cottages created back then are still in use today, retaining their rustic charm. Many older structures have been added to and upgraded by new generations or new owners. Floor plans tell the tale of accretion, leaning new additions onto old, adding new plumbing and electrical work, and brightening up the interior with more windows and skylights. Yet at their core there may still be a great gathering space and majestic fireplace with a charred mantel highlighting the holiday fire of 1938.

But for many others, the search for a family cabin is relatively new and the structures created reflect 21st century life. Nowadays, they are rarely summer-only cabins but rather year-round retreats. Cabin-goers of today have brief interludes of vacation or long weekends (rather than a whole summer), and owners are dual-wage earners.

New structures often carry the promise of extended stays in retirement years. Empty-nester homeowners are selling the family home in exchange for an urban condo and a cabin. Such cabins become the repository of family heirlooms, photo albums, and family gatherings. But unlike city homes created for resale, family cabins are created to highlight family attributes, mindful of their role as a legacy structure.

In two of my previous books, *The Cabin* and *Back to the Cabin*, I focused on tiny to modest cabins. Here, in *The Family Cabin*, structures are explored in a greater range of sizes from modest to grand, though it's really less about size and more about the living experience. While several cabins are intended to sleep but a few, others are designed to serve multiple families and friends. Are they cabins or camps, lodges or lake homes? Their owners provide the answer when they exclaim in unison, "We are off to the CABIN with our family and friends for the long Labor Day weekend."

The family cabins presented here range in size, shape, color, and building method, in locations stretched across North America on mountaintops, near streams and lakes, in forests, or even in someone's backyard. I'll present the cabins in six categories, though in truth there's a degree of overlap among the categories and each would be capable of fitting other categories as well.

Cabin porches retain our connection to fresh air and the sounds of nature.

Camps, Cottages, and Cabins: What's in a Name?

What you call your modest retreat hidden away in nature has more to do with location than with the attributes of the structure you are retreating to. If you are in the Southwest, Midwest, or West, you are likely to use the name *cabin*. If you live along the seashore or in the Great Lakes region, you might say *cottage*. But if you are located in New England or the Adirondacks, you would use the term *camp*. All three names describe pretty much the same thing.

Early respites in nature were simply referred to as "camping" and occurred in tents, some permanently on platforms. As tents were replaced with more permanent structures, they became known as camps. Although we think of camps as an enclave of buildings, the word can also refer to a single structure.

History Lessons

Family cabins draw heavily from history either by actually recycling historical structures or by employing historical precedents in the design of new cabins. Some borrow from vernacular images of sheds, barns, or other small structures, while others recycle material from such structures. A few cabins borrow from the original aesthetic as additions are accreted over time.

Early American settler cabins, no longer viable at their current locations, are sometimes dismantled and reassembled into family cabins at new sites. Placed on new foundations and with modern additions, these will serve generations to come.

Cabin plans from earlier generations can serve as the genesis for new structures. Modified to include contemporary services, they connect yesterday with tomorrow. Some older cabins with charming character worthy of retention need only minor alterations to sustain their appeal.

For Everyone a View

Views to snow-capped mountains, across meadows of grazing cows, or over lakes or rivers have long been an attraction for family cabins, and their designs reflect it. Their rooms may stretch along a lakeshore or be collected on a promontory with views in many directions. Modern cabins use expanses of glass for both near and far views.

Linear plans allow all the rooms in a cabin to have the best possible views. On sloped sites, multiple levels take advantage of the views, with service and utility spaces tucked back against the hillside. Views to mountains are more likely to necessitate vertical assemblies of windows, whereas lake views require horizontal arrangements to capture sunset horizons.

Nature's Bounty

The unique beauty of rich natural settings is usually what first attracts us to a future cabin site. Projects featured in this section draw ideas or materials directly from the land. Family stories are often uniquely connected to these sites and may have been nurtured for decades and across

The warm glow of shelter draws us inside for food, family, friendship, and rest.

generations. For some families, a connection to the land began as a camping experience or a stay at a resort nearby. Buying a property often begins an odyssey, with investments made over time or in one fell swoop.

Respect for the land has directed low-impact development with the goal of treading lightly on the earth. A predilection for remote-access sites on islands or across streams has led to cabins built with small lightweight components easily transported by snowmobiles, boats, or small all-terrain vehicles.

Pier foundations help to preserve tree roots close to construction. Trees removed are milled for lumber in cabin interiors, and exterior wood siding is either left to weather natural gray or stained to match surrounding tree bark.

Nature's cabins are often off-grid, relying on passive or active solar orientation for warmth and electricity. The sound of loons, babbling streams, or the chopping of wood is preferable to that of electric generators.

Nestled Together

An encampment of family structures can often be created with shared land, trails, beach, or even a common dining hall. Or a single family might construct a hamlet of cabins focused around a main social and dining structure. Some larger cabins with multiple sleeping accommodations are created as a hamlet of cabins under a single roof.

A few cabin compounds have been created by development companies as a part of larger communities with diverse amenities. Other cabin compounds are the result of a collection of family and friends with a shared vision. Many have been in existence for generations, and new ones are still being developed. Sharing may begin only as a collective vision, but legal provisions are also necessary

Each cabin location has its particular set of colors with seasonal variation.

to ensure that change, maintenance, and use patterns retain common agreement over generations.

Fun and Functional

Family cabins are often created with limited resources and therefore tend to be frugal and functional. But this has not deterred designs from also being fun, reflecting the casual and personal proclivities of their owners and builders. Their designs also highlight the importance of togetherness, where privacy gives way to family interaction.

Through the introduction of unexpected color, evocative form, open interiors, and infusion of light, fun family cabins can provide us with environments that enrich our soul. When attached to natural settings promoting outdoor activities, these unique getaways are the antidote to a stressful lifestyle.

Prospects for the Future

Like all residential structures, family cabins can be the incubator for new building technologies or explorations of new spatial arrangements. They may transform existing structures in innovative ways. Cabins have a long history of being low-tech and off-grid, but new techniques and equipment make it possible to have modern conveniences at remote sites.

Their remote sites have also led to exploration of prefabricated panel or box structures. Fabrication can occur in a factory miles away, and assembly at the site may take but a few hours or days. And some prefab cabins come fully outfitted with furnishings, so all you need to bring is your fishing pole.

That said, let's go to the cabin!

History Lessons

A recycled two-century-old log cabin from nearby provided the core of this Virginia guest-house. The chimney stone is from Pennsylvania.

WHEN I FIRST SAW the log cabin perched along a hillside across an open meadow from the main house, I immediately thought of an English "folly." This term was common to country squires

A Cabin with a History

who sought a charming, modest structure to gaze upon while sipping an afternoon tea on the terrace. In this bucolic Virginia setting with cows grazing the meadow, I reflected back on the Duke of Bedford's thatched cottage at Endsleigh in Devon, England, situated picturesquely on the Tamar River. It is not that the buildings look alike, but both grace the landscape with their presence and are structures of humble beginnings.

TOP Shortleaf pine logs, fresh chinking, and longleaf pine ceiling beams lend rich character to the living room.

ABOVE The window trim is recycled paneling from the original cabin, while the mantel reuses chestnut wood salvaged from the sharecroppers' house that was removed from the site.

Brad and Martha's project began as a desire to replace two old tenant houses on their property that were beyond repair. As they contemplated a replacement, they happened upon the demolition of another tenant house a few miles away. As old siding was being stripped away, a charming log cabin was revealed. It inspired Martha, and she approached the demolition crew to learn more.

She met Meade Shirley of Elk Mountain Contracting, who regularly finds value in structures that others would throw away. Many old barns, sheds, and houses are more valuable as a cache of reclaimed lumber, and a few can be moved intact. Some are precious, as was Martha's eventual purchase, and can be dismantled and reassembled.

Meade believes the logs of the cabin are of old-growth long-leaf pine. Counting rings on a few of the larger logs suggests that the trees were 200 years old when felled. A found copy of the original deed indicates that the cabin was likely built around

A moonrise, the Milky Way, and the Northern star are potential highlights of a twilight gaze from the north-facing porch.

Stairs to attic bedroom

Kitchen

Living room

Deck

Porch

MAIN LEVEL

N

Bedroom

Bedroom

Patio

LOWER LEVEL

1828. Doing the math, that means the pinecones that produced this fine structure started their journey nearly four centuries ago.

Meade was happy that the cabin would find a new home a few miles away and in the same county. There was also symmetry in the fact that the structure had once been home to a country doctor, and its new owner, Brad, is also in the medical profession. "We are just delighted to have found something this old," says Brad. "There are a thousand imagined stories in this structure."

As the project moved forward, they enlisted architect and neighbor Bahlmann Abbot to develop the floor plans. Wanting to retain the footprint of the original, they were able to accommodate a three-bedroom cabin on three levels: Two new bedrooms and a bath comprise the lowest level; living, dining, and kitchen are on the main level; and a bedroom and bath are in the upper attic space.

The original logs were numbered, dismantled, and reassembled on Martha and Brad's land. A few rotted logs were replaced

TOP LEFT Each lower-level bedroom has patio access and a meadow view.

OPPOSITE A compact kitchen is all that's needed for guests. The cabinets and flooring are pine recycled from an old factory in southeastern Virginia.

Log Joinery

We typically think of log structures as having corners where the log extensions occur in an alternating pattern. These are often referred to as "saddle and notch" corners and are similar to the toy Lincoln Logs® we assembled as children.

Meade Shirley refers to the joinery used in the cabin that he dismantled and reassembled as "V-notch"; it has no log extensions. Together with dovetail-cornered joinery, these squared-off corners have the advantage of facilitating a refined future exterior of clapboard siding.

Log structures were often deemed primitive in a pejorative manner. Overlay cladding was thought to be of higher stature and could be added years after the log structure was built. This cladding has preserved many cabins that are now being repurposed.

with timbers from a depot in Maine. "Typically with these types of projects we have to determine how authentic the cabin should be and how that can accommodate the owners' needs," notes Meade. "Here we used many of the original materials, trim, flooring, brick, doors, etc. The reclaimed wood installed in the new portion of the construction really ties it together."

The original house on the site was demolished but provided chestnut for the fireplace mantel and stone for exterior retaining walls. Floor joists for the second story were reclaimed from a shipyard in Hampton, Virginia. The white oak for the exterior porches was cut on a farm in Appomattox, Virginia. The cabin is now occupied with guests throughout the year, including a short-stay schoolteacher and a recent family bridal party. "Occasionally we'll just walk over and have a cocktail on the porch," says Martha of her folly. "But most of all, I really like looking at it from our home. It puts a smile on my face, especially when the lights twinkle at dusk."

ABOVE Martha enjoys seeing lights on at her guest cabin across the meadow. It's a beacon of friendship.

LEFT Guests can relax on the covered porch, which has a view north to the Blue Ridge Mountains. The porch posts were sleeper joists in the original log cabin; the porch floor is locally sourced oak.

An ensemble of diverse log cabin components is tied together by a common wood stain, red roofs, and a stone plinth.

WHEN A CABIN IS BLESSED with enough original character, even if it's added onto again and again, the original aesthetic is never diluted but delightfully expanded. It's akin to a good jazz

The Camp That Keeps on Growing

performance, where the theme holds everything together as additional instruments come into play. We might call this a delightful accretion, or simply enriching a theme.

Such is the case with the Albinson/Mulheran lake cabin in central Minnesota that started life in 1939 (see the drawing on p. 25). The Albinsons created a modest 420-sq.-ft. one-room structure with a sleeping loft over the

The sleeping loft above the kitchen and the red countertop were in place early in the evolution of this cabin. New knotty pine is matched seamlessly with the existing paneling.

kitchen. It was clad in half-log siding and featured a fieldstone fireplace and an interior of rich knotty pine.

By today's standards, it was a primitive place served by an outhouse 30 yards away. A sand-point water well provided drinking water via a hand pump at the kitchen sink. Heating and cooking were done with woodstoves, and lighting was from kerosene lamps. By 1951, the Albinson family had matured, and it was time to add a boathouse with a sleeping room above for their two boys.

Modernization came in 1971 when a bathroom, bedroom, and storage room were added along with running hot and cold water to the kitchen sink. Three generations of the Albinson family enjoyed life in these structures at Bay Lake for nearly 50 years.

Dan and Carol Mulheran discovered the beauty of the same lake in 1981 while dining along its shores at a local resort. "They walked us into the lodge dining room and sat us down

LEFT A boathouse with guest sleeping above boat storage is a treasured getaway, especially for a younger generation who might enjoy a midnight dip in the lake.

ABOVE Beach sand and grass clippings can be washed away outdoors before entering the cabin. The shower is located on the back side of the boathouse, convenient for swimmers and boaters.

at a table in front of the windows and the scene took our breath away," notes Dan. "It was one of those idyllic nights—about 7:30 p.m.—the lake was calm, the sun was glowing out of the west, and a single boat was plying the waters." They booked a week for the next summer, then the summer after that for two weeks.

By 1987, the Mulherans had decided to search for a place of their own and boated the lakeshore looking for opportunities. Their realtor told them of a new listing he was hoping for: "It's a nice little log cabin with a boathouse that faces south." They surreptitiously discovered the boarded-up Albinson place and over the next couple of months acquired the rights to their dream cabin. By August 1988, they began a cleanout and a move-in to what would become decades at the lake.

They immediately set about adding 3 ft. to the bathroom with space for a tub and linen chest and added a laundry and

ABOVE A screened porch is attached to the guesthouse just across the deck from the main cabin. It's a perfect place to take a nap on the porch swing.

RIGHT Even the log-storage shelter matches the camp aesthetic. It's along the path to the garage, which has additional sleeping space above.

mudroom behind the kitchen. They also upgraded the kitchen with new appliances and cabinets utilizing the same knotty pine mini-logs that the original 1939 cabin had been lined with.

For the next several years, small investments were made in a driveway, bunk beds, and a swimming dock. Dan reflects that "summers were spent in all manner of fun activities: swimming, water-skiing, tubing, horseback riding, go-carting, and endless hours of bridge with our kids around the dining room table." The children imported cousins and friends to join them, which began to put pressure on their meager accommodations. And as the children matured, it became time for gender separation and privacy.

In 1994, a guesthouse was added with bedroom, bath, and a screened porch. A breezeway deck connected the guesthouse to the main cabin. To ensure aesthetic continuity, this project

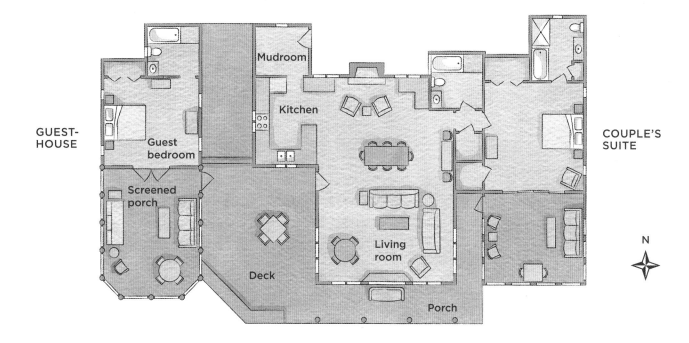

GUEST-
HOUSE

Mudroom

Kitchen

Guest
bedroom

COUPLE'S
SUITE

Screened
porch

N

Deck

Living
room

Porch

was constructed by the son of the contractor who had built the boathouse/bunkroom for the Albinsons 43 years earlier. By 2001, a new couple's suite seemed in order, replacing the 1971 bedroom addition that the Albinsons had made. A basement was added at the same time, and the whole cabin was outfitted with an insulated foundation.

Now a centralized furnace was possible, and seasonal use of the cabin greatly expanded. The Mulherans also added a new garage for storing water toys and above it a sleeping attic. This brought their collective sleeping capacity to 16, just in time for the arrival of children's spouses and future grandchildren.

In 2004, the family needed to address a decaying boathouse, so they set about restoring it. The stone base they added was so charming that, two years later, they decided to continue the theme on the main cabin and bunkhouse. Finally, in 2010, the Mulherans decreed, "We're done!"

A fire pit near the beach is ready for sing-alongs, s'mores, and plenty of tall tales.

Knotty Pine

Camp Mulheran has a rich interior composed principally of knotty pine walls and ceilings with accents of red on the countertops, lampshades, and chair upholstery. Knotty pine was a common, inexpensive material for early cabins and remains readily available today. Pine forests are abundant in many states across the United States and are regularly harvested and milled into variable board widths.

Knotty pine gets its name from the abundance of discernible knots in each board. The knots represent growth of the trunk around perpendicular limbs. Pine trees have many limbs, and when harvested and cut into boards the knots are visible and prevalent. Oil-based finishes and the long-term impact of ultraviolet light further highlight the knots.

As an interesting aside, in the 1950s, Formica® advertised its countertops in a knotty pine kitchen under the title "Knotty but Nice."

Not quite! In 2016, they realized that 16 beds and three generations were taxing their main living space, so they set about expanding that, too. There was no question as to what it would look like. The original palette of half-log siding, log columns, fieldstone elements, red roof, and knotty pine interior had served well to guide over three-quarters of a century of building, so why change a good thing?

HISTORY OF ADDITIONS

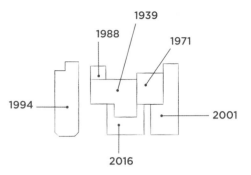

ABOVE The Mulherans boated by this cabin 30 years ago and thought how great it would be to own such a beautiful place as a retreat for their family. Now dreams and memories intertwine.

RIGHT Glaciers rolled these rocks millennia ago—just to make them ready for landscape walls.

A timber-framed living room silhouettes the chimney with its mix of sandstone, granite, limestone, and white rock, all recycled from the foundation where the original cabin had stood.

A YOUNG FAMILY'S FIRST foray into nature in search of a bonding experience and a break from city life is often to go on a camping trip. That was certainly true for Jake and Carol, who

Peace Cabin

discovered a perfect slice of nature on the edge of the Ozarks in the Mark Twain Forest in Missouri. It was only two hours' drive from their home in Columbia and an easy weekend or longer escape for their family of six. With camper in tow, they returned often to the joys of swimming, canoeing, and campfire songs.

By 1993, ownership of a little slice of heaven became a priority, and when 47 acres of an old homestead became available, they quickly drove to see it. Carol could immediately see that Jake

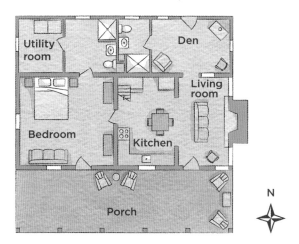

ABOVE A steep stair leads the way to a loft and guest bedroom. The floor joists were salvaged from a dismantled grain elevator in the region.

was enthralled, so she said, "Sign us up." Now they owned a hilltop, a meadow, a stream bank, and plenty of forest with lots of camper parking possibilities.

An old homestead foundation lay in ruin in the meadow with just enough remaining to convince Carol that a home had once stood there. She began to picture a settler's log cabin—though the one in her dreams had running water, indoor plumbing, electricity, and a refrigerator. In short order, Carol and Jake were introduced to the log structure preservation work of John Ming.

John had just begun a business saving Missouri log buildings by dismantling them and selling the logs for reassembly on other Missouri sites. He was on a mission to retain their history in regional proximity to their original context. "I don't do this for the money," says John. "I do this for the fun of it and saving history. This is hard, dirty work, but there isn't a day that I don't come out here and enjoy it."

For Jake and Carol, John had an 1850s farmhouse he was dismantling only one county away from their new property. The core of the house was a 17-ft. by 29-ft., two-room log structure of black walnut. A 9-ft. addition ran along one side and wrapped around one end. The addition, also old, was

LEFT A deep porch serves both as entrance and outdoor living space. Beyond the trees is a gurgling stream to serenade along with the cicadas—unless you bring your own harmonica.

Repurposing Log Structures

Many original settler cabins remain buried inside clapboard walls on the outside or plaster walls on the inside. Having been well protected for many years, they remain prime candidates for repurposing as vacation log cabins. They require a significant amount of labor to be uncovered, numbered, disassembled, transported, reassembled, and have new chinking added. But unlike new log structures, these historical relics carry stories, character, and lore. Notches tell tales of where floor joists used to be, sliced fins for plaster to adhere to, and marked tails where the cabin's first assembly was catalogued.

ABOVE The fireplace lintel came from the builder's great-grandfather-in-law's barn foundation. The infill brick between the framing members on the entry wall is recycled from an 1835 schoolhouse, using a method known as "nogging."

RIGHT Nestled under the roof, a sleeping loft overlooks the living room and a guest bedroom.

composed of vertical timbers with a stone rubble infill. On the opposite long side ran an open porch.

The rubble wall was demolished and the logs and timbers numbered and dismantled for shipment to Jake and Carol's site. General contractor Larry Pilkenton was hired to prep the site and help John with the reassembly process. He would also put on the new roof, wire the house, and add Carol's plumbing. "Larry was brilliant," says Jake, "for weaving the plumbing into the log structure. And he even was able to flip the stairway so as to arrive above with ample headroom."

In the reassembly, Jake and Carol chose to highlight the timber-framed end space, leaving the intermediate floor out and adding a majestic fireplace and a loft overlook. They not only added a bathroom but two of them to accommodate the large gatherings of the family clan.

Jake and Carol bought the logs in 2002, but it wasn't until Christmas 2005 that they finally had a cabin worthy of guests. Now more than a decade later and with nine granddaughters in the family, it is a favorite place for reunions and special holidays.

TOP LEFT The den opens to the living room, which in turn opens to the porch. The timber frame is walnut and was numbered with Roman numerals when originally assembled.

ABOVE The guest bath off the den doubles as they main floor powder room. The flooring was recycled from an old area school and had children's initials carved into it.

Glass doors and a lakeside deck open this 90-year-old cabin
to the water and summer sunsets.

SOME OLDER CABINS HAVE so much charm and such strong familial memories that any thought of change seems abhorrent to their owners. Such was the case for this family cabin in north-

Welcoming Cabin

western Minnesota. Although the kitchen had always felt isolated from cabin life at the owners' beach and disconnected from their cozy living room, any discussion of change was quickly voted down. How could anyone contemplate taking a crowbar or saw to their revered knotty-pine living room just to open up a view?

John and Susan had purchased the cabin in the mid-1980s, co-owning it with good friends Tom and Barb.

ABOVE A treasured living room with its charming split-rock fireplace remains largely intact except for the openings to the kitchen and porch. The columns carry the original roof load and at the same time frame the kitchen island.

LEFT The white kitchen reflects morning light deep into the dark-wood living space. Guests can chat with the chef yet remain out of the way of the kettle of boiling fish stew.

ABOVE Across from the kitchen is a banquet dining space wrapped in knotty pine. What was a door has now been opened above the bench end walls.

Their collective five children had grown up summering at the lake, learning to swim, fish, ride horses and bicycles, and to negotiate with each other. They grew to love returning each summer to the lake cabin and its relaxed rhythms of life. Susan, Barb, and the children were in residence for the whole summer, which was filled in part with teaching their children the arts, biology, and even French lessons.

Change began in the mid-1990s when Tom and Barb bought the cabin next door and the children moved into their college years. Summer jobs and foreign travel disrupted the patterns such that lake time now came in the form of a week or two here and there rather than a couple of months at a stretch.

Tom and Barb's cabin had the same challenge of an isolated kitchen, and they hired me to address the issue. Our solution was to create a plan that opened the kitchen to the living room and then opened the living room to the porch so that all could see the water beyond. The new functional kitchen with fir walls and cabinets was well crafted and soon felt as if it had always been there. In weekend visits with my friends Tom and Barb, I often discussed the prospects of a similar scheme for John and Susan's cabin.

After seeing the harmonious success at the cabin next door—and now knowing they had both a sympathetic builder and an empathetic architect in hand—John and Susan were willing to cautiously address their isolated kitchen. Retirement was on the horizon and a new generation of grandchildren in prospect, so John and Susan decided a fresh new kitchen was in order. Grandparents' instincts demanded that they be able to see the young cherubs heating their mac n' cheese.

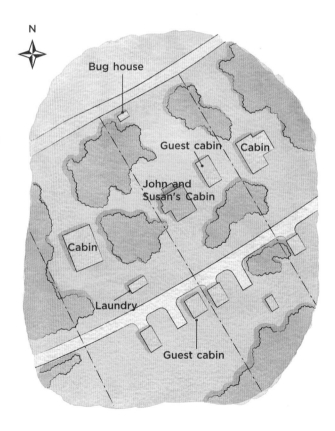

N

Bug house

Guest cabin   Cabin

John and
Susan's Cabin

Cabin

Laundry

Guest cabin

ABOVE A lone post remains where a wall once stood as the space is opened across the porch to the view.

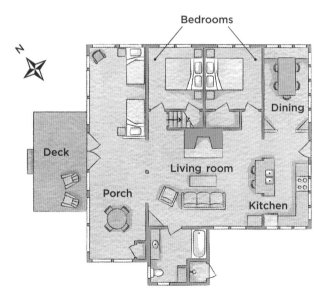

Our scheme opened walls on either side of the living room, connecting kitchen, living, and porch to the lake view. The high ceiling of the living room left ample wall surface above the 7-ft. openings. Columns that were needed to bear structural loads all helped retain the living room character as if acknowledging the wall that had once been there. Opening up the southeast kitchen helped bounce light into the previously dark room.

French doors were added from the porch to a new deck on the lakeside. The low glass in the doors accommodates beach viewing, even for anyone slouched on the living room sofa. And the deck is John's favorite place to unwind with a cocktail before a sunset view in the evening.

John and Susan's beach remains the communal hub, not just with Tom and Barb but also with several other families along the shore. And now Susan can spot early-bird arrivals all the way from her kitchen sink. A screened-porch gazebo, "the bug house," adorns the shore and is a favorite spot for birthday parties, 4th of July picnics, or just relaxing with a book at dusk.

At the Lake

Minnesota lake cabins built in the early part of the 20th century provided basic summer living near the lakeshore. The porch was the prime place for water viewing and cool breezes, with living rooms and bedrooms tucked behind. Living rooms featured a fireplace for cool days and evenings. Kitchens with their hot wood-burning stoves were at the back of the cabin, convenient to the hand pump outside and a back porch containing the icebox. Food preparation began outside, whether snipping the beans, husking the corn, or cleaning the fish.

Twenty-first-century lake cabin residents expect water views from all possible rooms for the visual benefit of their reduced vacation time. An open plan with modern conveniences, which wouldn't have been recognizable 75 years earlier, fits the casual lifestyle of contemporary families.

A screened-in gazebo at the beach, affectionately called "the bug house," is a community meeting room.

A thicket of low blueberry clumps in the near-treeless foreground is in keeping with the windswept character from which this family cottage gets its name.

"I WISH TO SAY at the outset that the setting of this novel has no exact location on any exact portion of the coast of Maine. Windswept is a wholly fictitious house placed in eastern

Windswept

Maine, anywhere between Schoodic Point and Passamaquoddy." So wrote Mary Ellen Chase in the foreword to her 1941 novel *Windswept*. This statement may be one of the greater fictional notations in her novel, for indeed Windswept is real. Chase may have sought to retain her reclusive privacy at Windswept, or perhaps she was using discretion for the Daniels family from whom she was renting the cottage. The instant success of her novel provided her the means to

ABOVE A weathered shed along the path from driveway to cottage shows the effects of years of exposure to the natural elements.

purchase Windswept the following year, and it remained her summer residence for the next 15 years. In 2007, the cottage was placed on the National Register of Historic Places—not so much because of its outstanding architectural merit but because it was the lead character in her novel of the same name.

In addition to Chase, the cottage, which was originally built in the 1920s, has seen several owners. It was on the market in a rather run-down physical state when Mark and Wellner dropped by in December 2009 to check it out. "We immediately fell in love with it in spite of the fact that the fireplace didn't even work," notes Wellner. The cottage was not on a proper foundation, and its principal inhabitants were mice.

Part of what makes Windswept so attractive is its spectacular site. Set in a field of blueberry clumps, it is on a promontory with a commanding ocean view. Even in a low, dense fog with the distant sound of foghorns, it is truly memorable. Chase said of the site, "Although some days were calm and soundless and the dark brooding land seemed asleep, on most the wind was strong and ruthless…. We will name the place Windswept."

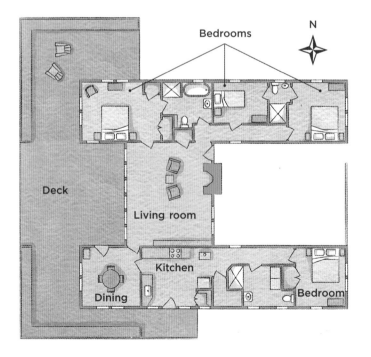

ABOVE The west-facing deck allows panoramic sunset views of the undulating Maine coastline.

LEFT The wall of new windows in the living room yields ample light and ventilation—whether for a watercolorist or a gathering of the family.

TOP The kitchen is convenient to a wraparound outdoor deck or the dining room. Reflections of Mary Ellen Chase cooking here are just for the imagination.

ABOVE The living room fireplace was totally dismantled and the stones sandblasted and then reassembled.

By the summer of 2010, Mark and Wellner had discovered area architect Robert Knight and embarked on a major restoration project. Bob comments, "What do you keep and what do you throw away? The building had no foundation, no insulation, exposed plumbing, wildly dangerous wiring, lovely but decrepit windows. Our clients wanted a usable house, ideally one that could be used year-round, but they had no ambitions to change anything for the sake of change. Nice starting place for working on a house that is on the National Register."

The structure was rolled off its rotten piers, a new insulated foundation was created, and then the structure was rolled back to the original site. The existing fireplace was dismantled, stone by stone, then the stones were sandblasted and the fireplace re-created. Studs and rafters were reinforced, and hurricane ties were added to anchor the structure to the foundation.

ABOVE The plumbing in the cottage had to be completely replaced with new fixtures and fittings that were in scale and character to match the existing design.

RIGHT The dining room has south and west windows with a north door to the deck.

In the Words of Architect Robert Knight

"Renovations interest me because you are joining something that is already happening, and may have been happening for a long time—so while there is room to insert new ideas, you should be singing along with the melody of the existing building, and it's fun to try and learn the melody."

"So what period do you go back to? I read *Windswept*, noting all the specific references to the house. It is this house that is the lead character in the book, and we decided that it would be our guide. So although the house is now almost entirely new, I think it is somewhat more faithful to the house that you would see in your mind as you read the book than the house we started with."

New windows were installed, and the house was replumbed and rewired. "All of this work was done over the winter with an amazing construction crew led by builder Gary Googins," notes Mark.

The cottage had faded white windows and trim when Mark and Wellner discovered it. But Bob thought otherwise. "The color change on the outside comes from the book, which talked about dark green trim, but also mentioned colors to match the sea nearby. We opted for a muted green to complement the weathered shingles."

By the summer of 2011, it was all back together and Mark and Wellner along with their two children began to enjoy cottage life there. "We are part of the great community out on the point," notes Mark. "We collectively celebrate Memorial Day weekend, the 4th of July, and Labor Day weekend with potluck dinners." Wellner helps with the cooking and is now known for the ginger cookies she contributes. I wonder if Ms. Chase would enjoy them?

ABOVE Working shutters, a necessity for this windy site, were rebuilt. The sea green window color was inspired by a reading of the *Windswept* text.

RIGHT The Fairy House is burrowed into the base of one of the site's few trees; it's a favorite spot for neighboring children and their rich imaginations.

Entry to Windswept is through a sheltered courtyard, graced by the rebuilt chimney.

The rebuilt porch cabin retains the communal gathering place
that Jenny sought for her family and beach friends.

THE SPIRIT OF A CABIN can be a potent force in a family's collective memories of summer days at the lake. For Jenny, her family, and descendants, the idea of a cabin was integrally tied to life

All about the Porch

on the porch. Eating, playing games, reading, socializing, and sleeping were all porch activities and only a stone's throw from the beach. All other rooms, which included the kitchen, bedrooms, and bathroom, were as if an appendage to the porch. Their cabin was central to an enclave of cabins and the prime beach location for all the neighboring cabin families. It wasn't just Jenny's cabin but at times "cabin central" for a herd of sandy feet and

ABOVE The attached structure (at right) is the original granary that was central to the old porch cabin. It was slid aside during construction and brought back as a guest space.

BELOW The interior of the granary, with sleeping loft above, is a popular hangout for neighborhood teens.

ABOVE The barn door conceals the pantry in this bright and colorful kitchen.

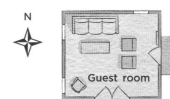

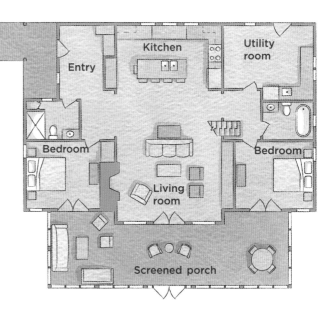

hungry stomachs. And even on a rainy day, the porch was the communal library of books to borrow.

The original cabin had started its life more than a century earlier as a converted granary moved to the beach from a neighboring farm. Jenny's great-grandfather, George Lowry, had the granary slid across the frozen lake pulled by a team of horses. Over the years, several additions had been made, with each addition leaning on the ones that had been made before. All additions were accessed through a long porch to the beach.

The site was on low ground on an isthmus of land between two lakes. A high water table had caused significant annual frost heaves, and the cabin was so out of plumb that Jenny's bed had to be made level by placing a full concrete block under one bedpost. Uncle Mark referred to the cabin as having "a serious deviation from the vertical." The fractured structure was difficult to seal up against rainstorms and varmint infestations. Jenny had determined it was time for something new and better but with the feeling and spirit of the porch cabin of her memories.

Porch cabins of yesteryear were created for summer use only, in an era when a mother took her children to the lake for the whole summer. In the 21st century, cabin time is parsed in smaller units and is extended across the full year. Fall walks through the colorful forest, quiet days of cross-country skiing, and spring observation of bird migration can now be added to the year of cabin enjoyment.

The upstairs is reached by an alternating-tread stair, which opens onto a bridge that connects the two bedrooms, each with a lake view.

The living room opens to the wraparound porch through an accordion door.

Swan Lake Club

Jenny's porch cabin is in a community of cabins known as the Swan Lake Club. Thirteen neighbors from nearby Fergus Falls, Minnesota, had bought 40 acres of lakeshore in 1884. At first, they used the property for picnics, swimming, and camping, but over time they began to build summer structures. The cabins are individually owned, but the land has remained in common.

Although rules are few, two have remained: No boating without life jackets, and no swimming without an adult present. Children are free to roam from one end of the camp to another and are welcome anywhere along the way. Conviviality has remained the spirit of the camp for more than 120 years.

Jenny's search for the right solution led her to my design work and writing on cabins. I had recorded several classic porch cabins in magazine articles and in two books. This led to my designing a few porch cabins, one of which is documented in my earlier book *The Getaway Home* (The Taunton Press, 2004). So it seemed a natural fit to help Jenny envision a 21st-century model of this classic typology.

When the old family cabin was demolished, the original granary was retained intact and slid off to the side of the site, while elevated fill was added to provide a stable building pad. A new more compact and partial two-story cabin was envisioned with the granary attached through a breezeway. It's used today as a teenagers' getaway and is likely to find diverse purposes over time.

A broad, narrow porch fronts the beach with two bedrooms and living space attached to it. Two additional bedrooms are at opposite ends of the second level, each with a lake view.

Jenny has now had a couple of years to test out her new porch cabin and to observe its patterns of use with various-size groups and in all four seasons. She has begun to rebuild the library collection to bolster the porch's role as the community room, and the fifth-generation children are well on their way to building porch cabin memories of their own.

For Jenny and her family, "cabin life is all about unplugging and unscheduling." Here, life is much unchanged from generations past. The children make trips to the candy store at Swan Lake Resort in the same little fishing boat the preceding Lowry generation used 30 years before.

ABOVE The upstairs south-facing bedroom has a modest deck for sunbathing, relaxing with a book, or overlooking the activity on the beach.

For Everyone a View

Located on a lake point, this century-old fishing cabin was transformed into a fresh contemporary getaway where new family memories could be forged.

"IT WAS A COLLABORATION," says Marian of the design for reconstruction of her Vermont cabin. "I brought whole binders of magazine cutouts that I had been collecting for years, doodles, and

Family Memories

notes, and designer Milford Cushman brought his fresh ideas, his amazing ability to synthesize, and his reverence for New England vernacular." Together they created a plan that stripped away the badly executed additions to the old cabin and created their own new additions and reorganized the feeling and flow of the place. At its core is a two-story atrium that brings focus to this family retreat.

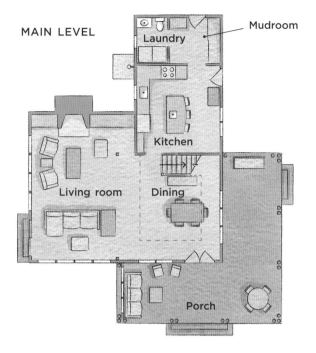

MAIN LEVEL

Laundry

Mudroom

Kitchen

Living room

Dining

Porch

UPPER LEVEL

N

Rumpus room

Bedroom

Atrium

Bunk room

Sleeping porch

Guest bedrooms

Marian had come to the project with a family history of connection to the neighborhood for as long as she could remember. Her grandfather had purchased land along the lake and over the years had subdivided it for various family members. She had spent countless summers there, intuitively knowing which glacial rock was the safest for diving, which picnic spot had the most glorious sunsets, and whose dock was a reliable source of slippery sunfish…and which candy at the local general store provided the best bang for the buck!

By the time she was married with three sons of her own, Marian knew she wanted to buy in and let the children experience a similar restorative lake life. But all the family lots were taken and likely to remain that way through heirs for many years to come. So when she heard that a particular old cabin in the neighborhood might be for sale, she walked the property and within about 10 minutes knew that she had to have the place.

The old fishing cabin had origins dating back to the early 1900s. It was 25 ft. from the shore and on a point with water and hillside views on three sides. Contemporary zoning rules mandated retention of the 1,556-sq.-ft. footprint, but with Cushman's imaginative solution, another 1,246 sq. ft. were added on the second floor.

The main level is divided into indoor and outdoor social areas and a utility core of kitchen, mudroom, and laundry.

RIGHT The cabin is long and thin, which brings light and fresh air to all the living spaces. The wraparound porch orients east and south.

FAR RIGHT Glass-fronted shelves in the kitchen make it easy for infrequent users to find what they're looking for.

ABOVE Dining al fresco with a panoramic view means there's not a bad seat at the table. The food will have lots of competition for attention.

ABOVE A wall of large sash windows allows a sunset view from the living room.

OPPOSITE The granite fireplace in the living room has a rough-textured finish. Glass and screen door closures stack to the side.

Unlike most cabins where kitchens are integral to social space, Marian sought a division between work, such as cooking and cleaning, and the space of relaxation and social gathering. Three walls of large windows and French doors give an airy, at-the-lake feeling to this social realm, which is separated from the kitchen by a pocket door.

An original two-story atrium with stair and catwalk links the social space to the four bedrooms above. Bedrooms are accessed and served by the catwalk, and an additional rumpus room can be reached off of the stair landing. The owners' three sons share a bedroom with its own loft, leaving two bedrooms for guests and the last bedroom as the couple's suite (complete with a narrow bath and private sleeping porch).

ABOVE The double-height dining space is flanked by the stair to four bedrooms above, which are reached along an overlook catwalk.

LEFT A bunk room is tucked under the eaves; a third bed lofted above the door is accessed by the ladder.

BELOW RIGHT A long, narrow bathroom attached to the couple's bedroom features a tub with windows on two sides in the principal viewing corner.

ABOVE Low windows below overhangs make for great bedside views. The painted space highlights the roof rafters for added character.

The central atrium provides great airflow, with warm air rising to the top and pulling the cool lake air into the social spaces below. A fireplace in the living room takes the chill off on cool fall evenings.

Marian and the boys live at the lake for the whole summer, and husband Greg joins for long weekends and one two-week stint. Although there's plenty going on at the lake all summer long, the highlight is the annual pig roast. The locally produced swine is marinated for three days in a special brew of regional ingredients including maple syrup and slow-roasted in a Cuban pig box.

After a busy summer with family and friends, Marian enjoys a quiet week in the fall all to herself. As a writer, she gets inspiration from the still water, the haunting calls of the loons, and the early sunsets.

ABOVE The morning sunlight casts a warm glow, awaiting the rising of the family for the day's activities at the lake.

BELOW The glass-enclosed west end protects the porch from cool winds.

The southern view from the screened porch has been
enjoyed by four generations of this New England family.

BASIL AND DIA ARE EXCITED about their new status as grandparents, especially when entertaining their family at their lake cabin in Maine. Four generations of Basil's family have now enjoyed the

Heavenly Haven

place his father purchased in 1951 and named "Porta Panagia." When translated from Greek, it means "Gateway to Heaven," and in its sunny setting with a lakeside beach and a backdrop of Eastern white pines it remains a heavenly haven for all.

Basil's father, Charles, built a seasonal structure on the lake, which was efficient and inexpensive. It was gradually winterized to make it available for skiing weekends but

ABOVE The cabin
stretches out
along the shore to
accommodate views
from all rooms on
three levels.

OPPOSITE The
interior woods of
pine, red birch,
white cedar, and
hemlock are a
palette drawn from
the trees of the site.

without proper vapor barriers to go along with the insulation. Mold and mildew began to surface, and with a new generation of the clan soon to arrive, Basil and Dia decided it was time to rebuild. With four children, some now married, and already three grandchildren, they needed both a bigger and certainly a better cabin.

They interviewed several architects for the task before settling on Rob Whitten from Portland, Maine, appreciating how he listened to their goals, integrated their ideas with his, and respected their setting in the pines.

Basil and Dia soon learned that there were zoning restrictions to size and location, measured in volume rather than footprint (see the sidebar on p. 68). Their old structure was noncompliant but would in part be grandfathered in. There was also a septic system regulation that limited the number of bedrooms they could have.

Rob set about designing a three-level structure banked into the hill. Bedrooms would be kept modest in size with the focus put on maximizing social space. All the rooms would

FIRST FLOOR

Down to lower level

Porch

N

Kitchen

Living room

Dining

Balcony

Bedroom

Screened porch

SECOND FLOOR

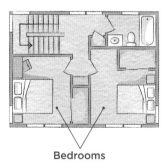

Bedrooms

ABOVE The fireplace, built from local stone, is the focal point of the living room and is visible from the kitchen and dining area.

have southern views to the lake, which would also provide passive solar gain in winter months. Locating the stair in the center of the floor plan reduced any need for wasted hallway space.

Plenty of storage was built in throughout the cabin to reduce clutter. The differing ceiling heights enhance spatial variety, with a flat ceiling in the kitchen, exposed joists in the dining room, and a vaulted ceiling in the living room and bedrooms. The high ceiling above the upper bedroom closet and bath accommodates a child's loft.

The interior materials are pine, red birch, white cedar, and hemlock, selected from the surrounding environment and commonly used in local cabin construction. Maine slate is employed on counters, and the fireplace stone is local, laid up by the son of the mason who built Basil's father's fireplace. The exterior was stained to blend in with the forest, and materials were selected for longevity and minimal maintenance.

Energy efficiency is gained from the hill embankment, from the trees to the north, and from the high-density foam insulation in the walls. Radiant heat is used in the lower-level floor, and the whole heating system can be monitored and controlled from the owners' city location. The Rumsford-style fireplace,

ABOVE A single window in the compact kitchen captures the view back to the driveway. The countertop is Maine slate, and the wood-clad ceiling is regional pine.

LEFT The screened porch and open deck reflect the character of the shoreline.

Zoning Limitations

Remote cabin locations are just as likely to have zoning restrictions as their city counterparts, and they are unique to their natural settings. This is usually the community's way of retaining the environmental quality of a locale. There might be both state and local regulations.

According to architect Rob Whitten, one of the challenges of building in the local Shoreland Zone is a minimum setback of 75 ft. from the highest annual water level, which means that no houses, decks, pools, or other structures can be built within this zone. The Shoreland Zone is measured from the highest annual water level to 250 ft. back. Here are some of the other limitations of Maine's Shoreland Zoning as it is applicable to Basil and Dia's property:

• The maximum lot coverage of nonpervious surfaces—roofs, walkways, driveways, decks, porches, etc.—is 20% of the total coverage of the area of the property in the Shoreland Zone.

• The maximum height of a structure (to the ridge) is 35 ft. above the existing mean grade of the site.

• You are not allowed to clear view corridors to the water.

• You can remove up to 40% of the existing tree cover over a 10-year period provided you adhere to a complicated system of points per tree size.

• You cannot open a tree canopy greater than 10,000 sq. ft. to accommodate a new structure, including septic systems.

• You are required to maintain a vegetative buffer of native species between the house site and water.

which is good for heat radiation, is fitted with doors for reduced heat loss.

"Building this cabin was a great experience," concludes Basil. "We came often during construction, getting to know the workmen. Mike Meyer and his Island Cove Building Company staff even drew a martini glass in the temporary kitchen bar they had installed. We knew then that they were kindred spirits."

Basil and Dia could not be happier with the results. Only two hours away from their year-round home near Boston, they frequent the cabin in all seasons. They wouldn't miss the local Maple Syrup weekend, the Fishing Derby, Greek Easter, or all the important holidays with their growing family.

LEFT A singular tree trunk greets guests to this family cabin, with ample roof covering above to set down luggage and food supplies out of the rain.

OPPOSITE Winding down the evening with some quiet time at the fire pit has been a favorite family pastime for decades.

A covered outdoor walkway connects all the rooms of this northern Minnesota cabin and captures the morning sunlight.

ARCHITECTS, BUILDERS, AND their clients typically share a healthy trust, established and reinforced during a series of meetings and reviews running the length of the design and

Trustworthy

construction process. Sometimes, however, that trust is based on little more than a handshake, a solid reputation, a terse set of instructions, and some well-placed faith.

Such was the case back in 1949, when a South Dakota family man, after vacationing near Ludlow's Island Resort on Lake Vermilion in Minnesota, asked Hod Ludlow, the resort's owner and builder of local repute, to design and build a cabin for him. He had purchased an east-facing lot on a quiet bay a short paddle

The dining table overlooks the patio and outdoor fireplace. Hod Ludlow crafted the rustic log lighting fixture over the table.

distance from Ludlow's Island. His requirements were few: Do it economically and expeditiously, and make sure all of the rooms face the water. The man then drove home 10 hours to Sioux Falls, South Dakota. A short time later, Ludlow mailed him a contract with assurances the cabin would be beautiful and ready the following summer.

Which it was—a lovely, motel-style structure where every room did in fact face east to the lake. Ludlow had discovered a flat, buildable plateau just above the water's edge and close enough to hear the lapping waves but protected by trees and a hill from the colder northwest winds. There was room for an ample cabin just a few steps from a boat dock. An old trapper's cabin on the property could be used as a bunkhouse for rambunctious teenagers or overflow guests.

Ludlow strung the cabin's five bedrooms, bath, kitchen/dining area, and living room along a covered outdoor walkway that afforded fresh air and an unimpeded view of the starlit lake on a midnight stroll to the bathroom. During waking hours, the walkway encouraged an outdoor lifestyle unusual even at a

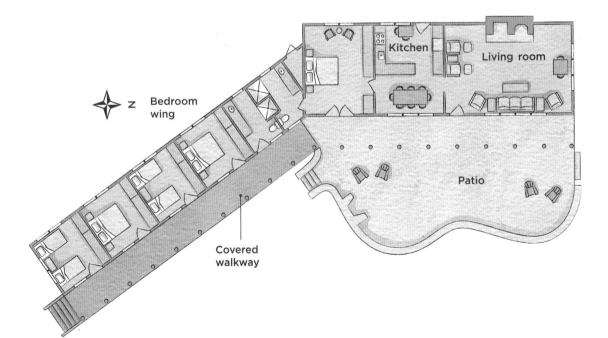

Bedroom wing

Covered walkway

Kitchen

Living room

Patio

ABOVE The ample living room with fieldstone fireplace is paneled in knotty pine.

LEFT The covered walkway serves well for drying beach towels and life jackets.

Each bedroom screen door carries a different cutout animal character to distinguish one room from another.

Northwoods retreat. The cabin features a handsome fireplace and a patio by local mason Ole Swanson, windows handcrafted by carpenter Charlie Pohl, and Ludlow's own rich detailing.

Vacation life centered immediately on the walkway and the adjacent terrace. Here the family communed with deer, chipmunks, and chickadees, beneath the occasional shadow of a passing eagle. They could also listen to the trolling fishermen debating whether the walleyes were biting. All in the bay knew when the family was in residence as brightly colored beach towels and a discordant array of life jackets all hung from the walkway portico.

Four generations have now enjoyed summers at the Vermilion cabin. The bond forged by the patriarch and the builder grew tighter when the former's son married one of Ludlow's daughters, Martha. It was she, by the way, who initiated one of the few changes made to the cabin in its 66 years: the addition of animal cutout cutting boards to the screen door of each bedroom. She had noticed that her daughter Ellen had tied a sock to her bedroom door so she could find her way back at night to the right bedroom. Since the doors all look alike, she reasoned, something was needed to tell the rooms apart. They could trust the iconic images to prevent confusion and even feel their unique shapes on a pitch-black night.

HOD'S BUNK BED

A Trusted Builder

Hod Ludlow had gained his trusted reputation not just by constructing structures that survived the harsh northern Minnesota winters but also by exhibiting a flair for inventive design. Near his resort, he built a stockade-style cabin with a cantilevered upper level and vertical log siding. At his resort, he created cabins where whole exterior walls were assemblies of doors, fixed in place. And at another small cabin, his response to an unlevel ledge rock was to have two small bedrooms sharing one bunk bed, the upper bunk reached from one room and the lower bunk reached from another.

A boathouse and covered boat slips are but a few feet from the end of the walkway. Martha's brother, Mark, remembers building a portion of the covering with his dad.

Martha's daughter, Mary, remembers the socks, but she also reflects on "the incredible gathering place of the patio. I wonder what the thought process was for Gumpy Hod in determining the angle for the breezeway. It is perfect, as you can be in the very last bedroom and still have a pulse of what is happening on the patio."

A few years ago, Martha received sole ownership of the property that she had cherished for its proximity to her extended family centered near the Island resort. Since her father's original masterpiece was intended solely for summer use, she recently has embarked on replacing the dilapidated trapper's cabin with a full-season guest cabin. With accessible features and an energy-efficient shell, she trusts both her late father and father-in-law would approve.

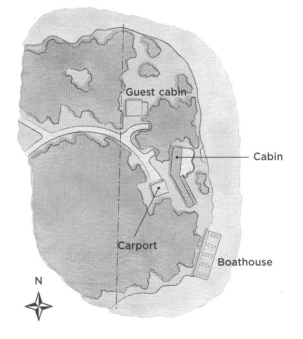

Guest cabin

Cabin

Carport

Boathouse

N

Banked into a North Carolina hillside, this cabin, which overlooks
a trout stream, was a dream of its owners for many years.

FLY FISHING IS AN elegant sport requiring skill, patience, and a willingness to scout out cool spring-fed streams. It is said to have existed in ancient Roman times and has been recorded in count-

In Search of a Mountain Cabin

less tales ever since. In 1653, Izaak Walton referred to fly fishing as "the contemplative man's recreation."

Sharon and Frank really got hooked on the sport at the beginning of the 21st century, long after Walton made mention of fly fishing in his classic, *The Compleat Angler*. According to Sharon, "There is a certain purity to fly fishing. There is the beauty of

From the entry across the kitchen to the screened porch, this cabin has an open, airy feeling.

standing in the middle of a stream and the challenge of trying to lure a perfectly adapted fish to your imperfect imitation of an insect." Sharon and Frank would escape from their home in Philadelphia in search of cool streams in the Poconos, White Mountains, or other locations along the Appalachian Ridge. They enjoyed their time together in the solitude of a stream and also in the small towns and country inns they discovered along the way.

After a decade of diverse explorations, they began to hunt for a permanent base camp for their fishing forays. They had settled on a 10-hour radius from Philadelphia, and with retirement in mind, they considered southern locations versus the northern options. The recreational area of Ashville, North Carolina, was within reach, so they began to look in earnest for appropriate property. They sought isolation, privacy, and nature but also considered cultural conveniences as well as security issues.

Sharon and Frank found several lots in a 3,000-acre conservancy near the town of Black Mountain in the Blue Ridge Mountains and hired Duncan McPherson of Samsel Architects to review the sites for buildability. They had interviewed five firms and concluded that Duncan's "not so big" approach resonated with their goals, aspirations, and budget. They let

On the Fly

Sharon and Frank were taught the art and science of fly fishing by Trout Unlimited, a national conservation organization. They principally fish limestone streams of eastern and central Pennsylvania and the streams of western North Carolina.

"We fish mostly the upper reaches for wild trout, meaning those that are naturally born and not stocked," notes Sharon. Brown trout and rainbow trout are imports to the eastern United States, whereas brook trout are native. Sharon adds, "All three are beautiful, sporting, and can grow to amazing sizes due to the abundance of insect life that thrives on these streams. All of our fishing is catch and release."

Windows wrap the living and dining rooms, connecting the indoors to nature. Spruce paneling on walls and ceiling and a maple floor keep the space light, warm, and cheery.

MAIN LEVEL

LOWER LEVEL

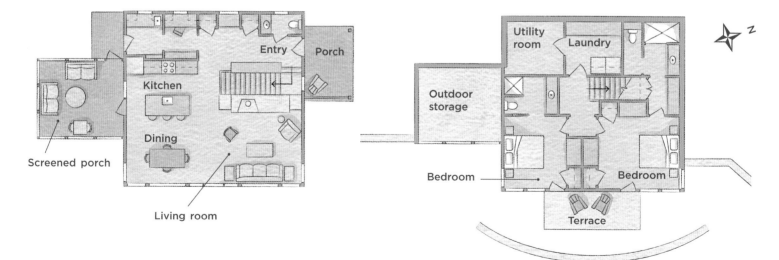

Entry

Porch

Kitchen

Screened porch

Dining

Living room

Utility room

Laundry

Outdoor storage

Bedroom

Bedroom

Terrace

N

Duncan know how the cabin should feel: harmonious with the land, cozy inside, and inviting in all seasons.

The lot they decided on would require a steep driveway and some retaining walls to create an adequate building footprint. This would place the cabin above the steady gurgling of the stream that they could see and hear in all seasons. They would be surrounded by forest rich in wildlife.

Sharon and Frank quickly began to learn of the unknown costs of well drilling, roadwork, foundation excavations, and bad weather construction. The property had been purchased in June 2012, but it wasn't until July 2014 that their cabin was move-in ready.

The Samsel design was for two levels, with the lower level banked into the hill. Bedrooms and utilities are below and walk out to the terrace. The entry and social spaces are on the upper level along with a screened porch on the south side. Generous windows on both levels look east toward the stream.

The open interior of the main level is wrapped in spruce with a clear finish, and the floor is a #2 hard maple. These pale-colored surfaces bounce light around, whether natural daylight or artificial light at night. The floating fireplace wall cascades down the stair in a rich wine red.

Efficient space planning and a well-insulated envelope helped the cabin meet the requirements of North Carolina's Energy Star® version 3. In-slab heating in the bathroom floor reduced demands on the heating and air-conditioning (HVAC) equipment. Low-maintenance exterior materials include prestained cedar shingles, aluminum-clad windows, and a Kynar®-coated steel roof, while the porch floorboards are local heat-treated ash.

A southeast view over the Adirondacks is just what the Wolcott family was looking for in their mountain retreat.

"WE COULD HAVE SELECTED land down in the valley by water or atop the mountain with a view," states Greg Wolcott. "Instead, we chose a view of Giant Mountain four miles away. We've gained a new appreciation for the dynamics of the sky. It is a nonstop show of weather diversity."

In the Treetops

Greg grew up in the Finger Lakes region of New York in a family that enjoyed camping, occasionally in the Adirondacks. That came to an abrupt end after high school when college and summer jobs got in the way. Some years later, Greg met and married Nancy, whose college years had included several Adirondack hikes. Soon a young family with two daughters, demanding jobs, and a move to Philadelphia consumed their lives.

Daughter Hillary made a friend whose family regularly vacationed in the Adirondacks. Eventually, Greg and Nancy were invited to join the friend's parents, and they became reacquainted with the beauty of the hills, forests, and clear blue lakes. They enjoyed the hiking and other

BELOW The covered entry punctuates the opening in the winged form to the mountain view beyond.

outdoor activities of mountain life and gradually developed an interesting community of friends there. It wasn't long before they were searching for their own little slice of heaven.

An ornithologist who lived in their mountain community decided to sell them a portion of his land that featured a spectacular view. And about this time, Greg and Nancy's daughter Tory was completing her graduate degree in architecture. Like many young architects before her, she would gain her first commission from her parents—who in turn would get a spectacular mountaintop cabin.

Nancy and Greg gave Tory three main directives for the project: It must blend in with the Adirondack character, with wood rather than steel or glass; it must be modest in scope and scale with just a few bedrooms and indoor and outdoor gathering places; and it must have a "wow" factor, apparent as soon as you walk through the door.

Tory's design is a horizontal wing that follows the contours of their hilltop prow. At its center is an open screened porch and deck (the wow factor). Connected by one continuous roof, the dogtrot-style floor plan affords the Wolcotts a smaller cabin for winter use in one wing and privacy for their guests

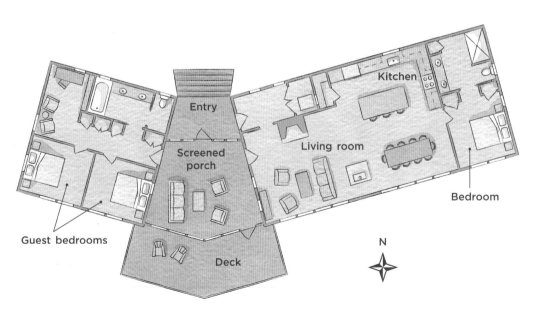

Entry

Kitchen

Screened porch

Living room

Guest bedrooms

Bedroom

Deck

N

The horizontal cabin spreads along the hillside under a canopy of metal roof.

in the summer in the other wing (see the floor plan on p. 84). "Essentially the cabin is a glorified lean-to," notes Tory, "with one shed roof building facing the valley and mountains beyond. The first goal of the design was to get the cabin out of the way, so to speak. This site is all about the view, being in the mountains, and enjoying nature. So I wanted the cabin to have a clean and simple form and to defer to its context as much as possible."

The view is to the south and southeast through a generous wall of glass. A deep overhang shades the summer sun but allows sunlight in for solar gain in other seasons. The walls, roof, and floor have extra insulation to sustain heat in cooler months. Cross ventilation and ceiling fans aid in summer comfort.

The whole family has enjoyed their mountain cabin, which they have named "Tree Top." For Greg and Nancy, now both in retirement, they balance two-week intervals at home and at the cabin. They have discovered the great markets down in the valley and take advantage of the excellent golfing and kayaking opportunities in the area. They are committed hikers who have hiked 39 of the 46 peaks of the Adirondacks. And the ornithologist who lives next door has introduced Greg to a whole new world of birding.

The Forty-Sixers

The Adirondack Forty-Sixers is an organization of hikers who have climbed all 46 of the highest peaks in the Adirondack Mountains, which range from about 4,000 ft. to 5,400 ft. The first to achieve all 46 climbs were the brothers Bob and George Marshall (along with their guide Herbert Clark), who accomplished the feat between 1918 and 1925.

In 1936, a club (the "Forty-Sixers of Troy") was formed, composed of others who had succeeded in the 46 climbs. The inaugural meeting of the Adirondack Forty-Sixers was in 1948. Today more than 8,000 climbers have achieved the goal, including more than 600 who have climbed all 46 peaks in winter conditions and are entitled to wear "Winter 46-R" badges. The club sponsors a publication (*PEEKS* magazine), social events, and educational sessions in climbing and camping along with outdoor skills.

ABOVE The kitchen countertops are local honed granite. Tory selected a paint color on the cabinets to blend with the countertops and set the kitchen apart from the rest of the wood-clad interior.

RIGHT A morning glow awaits early risers with their first cup of coffee.

OPPOSITE LEFT The cabin interior features pine walls, hickory floors, and fir trim. The paneling is oriented vertically, as specified by daughter Tory.

OPPOSITE RIGHT Each guest bedroom has ample light and ventilation, as well as treetop views.

Three generations of a South Dakota family have enjoyed life at the lake and the many water activities that take place there.

"**MOM CREATED MANY MOMENTS** for our family and was truly the matriarch of our clan. She hosted legions of cousins, friends, and kids at the lake, and I marvel at how she kept us all

Mother's Place

fed in the early days with a trailer-sized kitchen, a small refrigerator, and water hauled down 75 stairs." So begins Ann's eulogy of her mother a few years ago. "Dad gives Mom credit for convincing him to buy the cottage in the early '60s, and it was Mom who made it a touchstone for our family for 50 years."

Ann's family was from Aberdeen, South Dakota, and the lake cabin they bought was just an hour from home. Ann and her sister, Jane, grew up spending every summer at the lake

ABOVE With a wall of east-facing windows and a white interior, the living space retains its lightness even into the evening.

with their mom. "My brothers were in sports, so they stayed home with my dad during the week." She can remember seeing baby Janie bathed in a dishpan on the kitchen table and growing up to play endless games of Yahtzee® and Monopoly® on rainy days. They water-skied on calm mornings, did laundry at the laundromat, and basked in the sun all day long. And in high school, they worked at the restaurant at the lake.

As young men entered their lives, the place on the lake was the ultimate test of any further relationship. "Did they get it?" Ann says. "Could they water-ski, help with the dishes, and actually enjoy a game of Demons that Jane inevitably won?" Not surprisingly, Ann met and married Mark, who grew up at his family's cabin in Wisconsin.

Life moved on and eventually Jane and Ann each bought cabins on either side of their parents'. They collectively shared a large grassy point at the midpoint of the lake, with a great swimming beach on one side and a deep fishing hole on the other. Games of all sorts took place on the lawn, and children playing could easily be overseen from cabin decks along the hillside above the point. And children there were—three daughters for Ann and two for Jane, all with cousins and friends in tow.

MAIN FLOOR

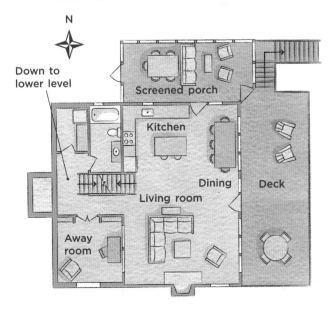

N

Down to lower level

Screened porch

Kitchen

Dining

Deck

Living room

Away room

UPPER LEVEL

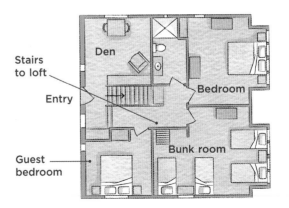

Stairs to loft

Den

Entry

Bedroom

Guest bedroom

Bunk room

ABOVE Sunrise has always been a favorite time for the family, whether for waterskiing, a morning swim, or just observing the tranquil lake.

RIGHT The north porch remains cool throughout the day, both for dining and entertaining neighbors.

Ann's Thoughts on the New Cabin

It's wonderful to work with clients who know what they want. Here are some of Ann's reflections on the work that we did together:

- Loved Dale's insistence to keep it a cabin, not a second home. Floors are ceilings since noise is a cabin thing. Bedrooms are open to lofts since privacy is not a cabin thing.

- One of the most influential suggestions he made that helped in planning was his comment that when he built his own cabin he limited his materials to only those things that could be bought at the local building center. Though we had to source some things in Minnesota, since South Dakota is more restrictive, this reminded us to keep it simple.

- Love that the design is what we call our old cabin grown up but not on steroids.

- Grateful we built it when the girls were still home and young enough to build memories in a new place.

- No closet doors, just cubbies with racks.

- No crawlspace, no critters.

- Away room . . . tiny but so much history there already as we crowd in 10 people for movies that work for all generations.

- Dishes and dancing in the same room.

The couple's bedroom is high under the roof, with eastern windows for an early wake-up.

Ann's children, now young adults themselves, reflect back on their own days of summer at the lake. "Every year around May, I would feel this inner tug—a call to the still mornings and glassy waters that bled into my daydreams, notebook doodles, song lyrics, and not-so-subtle conversations of how badly I needed a break from 'society,'" notes daughter Anna. "My friends never quite understood my unwavering devotion (until they were the lucky few who earned a visit) or why I was okay with 'missing out' on the summer flings, basement hangouts, and baseball 'superfanning,' but there was nothing that would make me miss my lake time."

Daughter Laura adds, "The cabin on the lake is our happy place. There is never any need for an alarm clock or a wristwatch. Each morning the sun beams in from the windows, illuminating every room in the cabin. Waking up to the natural light is one of

ABOVE The kitchen is on the middle level, just a few steps down from the entry for grocery arrival and a few steps above the dock level for serving the pontoon boat.

LEFT A functioning fireplace is a welcome option for cool fall evenings. The structural ceiling beams hold up the bedrooms above.

TOP The kitchen island is handy for breakfast for two, as well as for overflow dining from the larger table for big family gatherings. It's also a convenient spot for buffet serving to the porch, deck, or dock.

ABOVE The lowest level has direct access to the water, making it the natural location for storage of water-sport gear.

my favorite things as there is no timeline at the lake. Apart from weekly Sunday school, there is no particular place you have to be or errand you have to run. Each day is a new day, a blank canvas on which you can paint any picture you want."

In 2004, Ann and Mark decided their old, tiny cabin had seen better days and it was time to build something fresh and new, something without leaks or varmints. They wanted a taller cabin that would address the steep slope of their lot. And they wanted a screened porch for extended family outdoor living without the evening mosquitoes. They hired me to design it.

Entry to the cabin is now at the top level, where the family bedrooms are located. Down one flight of steps are the primary social areas of the living and dining rooms, kitchen, screened porch, and deck. There is also an "away room" for rainy-day movie watching or sleeping a guest. Below that at the lake level are a guest bedroom and plenty of storage for recreational gear.

A decade after it was built, daughter Elizabeth writes, "We still call our cabin the 'new cabin' even though it is 10 years old. The welcoming kitchen table, cozy away room, and heavenly screened porch never cease to amaze us. At least once a day, we tell each other how grateful we are to have our sacred space to share meals, play cards, or do dishes (and dance along the way). At the lake, we have an appreciation for small things we would never have noticed at home. A budding flower or a singing hummingbird is enough entertainment for a full morning. Cocktail hour, promptly at 5 p.m., consumes several hours of laughter before everyone realizes that they are hungry."

ABOVE Early morning light sets the cabin aglow.

LEFT The cabin is located on a point at the lake, so the deck captures panoramic views.

Nature's Bounty

Built with horizontal and vertical log walls more than
60 years ago, this simple Minnesota island retreat still
compels its owner to visit from Alaska every summer.

DEBBY DAHL EDWARDSON inherited the island cabin only recently from her late brother, Dave Dahl. "He loved this place, and he adored the man who built the fireplace," reflects Debby. "Carter

Island Cabin on Elbow Lake

Wetzel could do anything: cane chairs and snowshoes, fabricate diamond willow furniture, and create a fireplace with a special quartz rock strategically located. He became my brother's best friend and mentor on the lake, and they spent a great deal of time together."

Debby has been summering on a group of islands in this northern Minnesota lake all her life. From June to September, she'd spend all her time

here with her mother, while her father and two brothers would come on the weekends. "Mom was an artist, and I was a dreamy child who knew that place in the woods where the fairies lived and where I spent days creating things in the solitude that became a part of me, the solitude that makes me who I am."

Back then, she came to the islands from Minneapolis, just four hours away. Today, and for the past several decades, she treks from Barrow, Alaska, leaving her nest above the Arctic Circle for the balmy summers of northern Minnesota. She no longer has the luxury of a whole summer at the cabin but must make do with a few weeks here and there.

Debby married, raised seven children, and in those long, dark Alaskan winters became a writer of novels for young adults. She's thinking that her next novel might reflect her own youth on the lake, in this cabin and on this island, which is known today as Wee Toddy. She'll recollect her carefree teenage years boating to the resort to hang out with this week's city kids.

The 675-sq.-ft., two-bedroom cabin was built in 1953 for Don Macrae. The cabin's unique log style, with horizontal logs at the bottom below the windows and vertical logs above, was created by local carpenter Alex Olson. He was said to have been a small, happy, red-faced guy with a heavy Swedish accent and a penchant for alcoholic beverages. He was also an expert at constructing sunken crib docks, and several, including Debby's, have survived through 70 years of ice pressure.

LEFT A native fieldstone fireplace and local pine paneling fill the all-inclusive living space with rustic character.

RIGHT A trip to the outhouse is made utilitarian with an armful of firewood on the return.

ABOVE Once a sleeping porch, this tiny bedroom has just enough space for a bed and nightstand. The exterior logs are exposed on the left-hand wall.

Bedrooms

Living

Kitchen

N

Building with Logs

There's a logic behind Alex Olson's unique method of log construction, with horizontal logs at the base and vertical logs above. When logs are cut, they shrink in diameter but not in length. Thus, when stacked one atop the other, the whole wall shrinks, creating problems for doors, windows, and chimneys. By minimizing the number of horizontal logs to just enough to bond the structure together at the base, the shrinkage is reduced.

For the most part, the vertical logs correspond to the vertical dimension of the windows, ensuring that there's no vertical shrinkage where it would be most problematic. The smaller dimensions of the vertical logs would also have made it easier for Olson to hoist them into place.

Macrae's family sold the island to Dave in 1968, and Dave then proceeded to add an outhouse/woodshed/storeroom and a hot tub. For this work, Dave turned to local builder Chris Ikola, someone who was willing to tackle offshore construction. All the materials have to be brought across to the island by pontoon boat unless winter construction is preferred and the ice is strong enough for a pick-up truck. But then you have to contend with subzero temperatures and ferocious winds out of the north.

Electricity was brought to the island years ago, yet Debby still relishes her hand-pump water supply at the kitchen sink. Lake water supplies the hot tub, with the water heated by a wood boiler. Debby fires it up in the morning, and it is ready by evening for warm relaxation and a comfortable soak under the stars.

She reflects, "There is something about an island, something about waking in a log cabin to the sounds of loons calling and water washing over rocks. Something about those storms—the ones preceded by a strange, almost mystical silence in which the sky turns greenish yellow and the winds, when they come, come fierce enough to bend the tallest pines like grass. The storms that keep everyone off the lake save those of us on islands."

ABOVE There's always a need for books to read on an isolated island and space for mementos of seasons past. Doorways at left and right lead to the two bedrooms.

LEFT Summer mornings arrive early in this bedroom with east and south views. The pine walls will have seasoned to a warm honey hue.

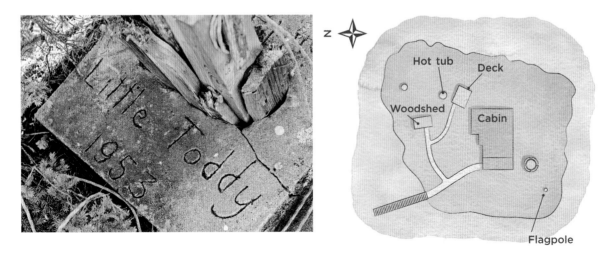

ABOVE Bathing in the hot tub might be a prelude to a brisk swim in the cold northern Minnesota lake . . . or the thaw afterward.

LEFT A concrete pad at the base of a flagpole carries the cabin name, Little Toddy, which stands on Wee Toddy island.

N

Hot tub

Deck

Woodshed

Cabin

Flagpole

A majestic wall of glass affords the Moffet family treasured views over the Canadian Rockies.

ARCHITECT PETER MOFFET retired from his Toronto architectural firm to a location across the country in the Monashee Mountains in British Columbia. Here, he and his wife, Linda, have settled

High Country Timber Frame

into some of the finest ski country in Canada, known for its focus on Nordic activities. "Our passion is ski touring," says Peter, "for the serenity of the landscape and the exhilaration of fresh powder."

There is also plenty of outdoor summer activity in the area, with hiking, horseback riding, and trout fishing high on the list. The site they selected is just outside the city of Rossland, known as the mountain

MAIN FLOOR

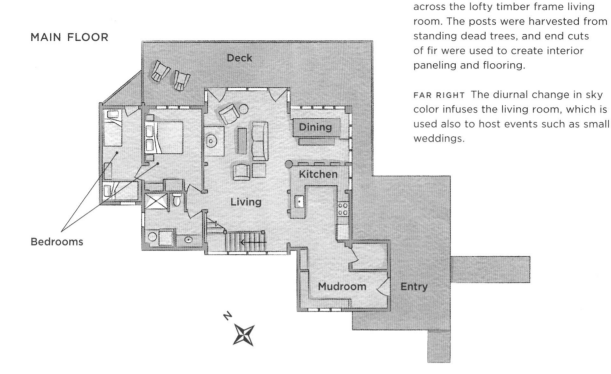

Deck

Dining

Kitchen

Living

Bedrooms

Mudroom   Entry

N

RIGHT Morning sunlight streams across the lofty timber frame living room. The posts were harvested from standing dead trees, and end cuts of fir were used to create interior paneling and flooring.

FAR RIGHT The diurnal change in sky color infuses the living room, which is used also to host events such as small weddings.

LOFT FLOOR

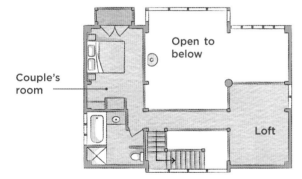

Open to below

Couple's room

Loft

bike capital of Canada. At an elevation of 3,400 ft., it enjoys cool summer days with low humidity.

The 5½-acre hillside site they purchased is heavily wooded in fir and pine. Access to the site is from above and opens to views to the northeast over the Columbia River valley and snow-covered peaks in the distance. Peter's design for their family cabin opens all rooms to the view on two levels.

The cabin is entered from the southeast through a mudroom with ample space for stowing winter gear. The main level houses an open living/dining/kitchen space, along with two bedrooms and a bath. The kitchen and dining area are located along the east wall to capture the early morning light. A stair rises up along a south wall of glass, flooding the living space with natural light in winter months. Upstairs, a bedroom and an open loft are connected by a bridge. In all, the compact plan contains about 1,500 sq. ft. of living space.

The cabin is built with materials that were locally sourced, processed, and manufactured, including Douglas fir, cedar, and slate. Salvaged logs and local standing dead trees were selected to reduce the impact on the environment. The fir logs were harvested within a 30-mile radius of the site and milled locally into timbers ranging in size from 2x4s to 8x12s. Interior paneling and exterior siding were processed from the timber cutoffs.

The furniture and millwork were also fabricated from local wood. The bathroom vanity is from old-growth cedar recycled from a dismantled bridge, while the dining room table was made from Douglas fir deemed too twisted to be used as construction lumber.

Since building the cabin a few years ago, Peter and Linda have added an 8-ft. by 12-ft. storage room for all of the outdoor gear that they have acquired. "I cannot seem to help

ABOVE A European woodstove rests on stone harvested from a local quarry.

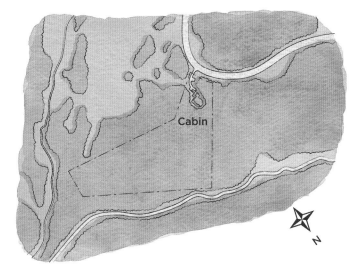

myself but to keep building," says Peter, who has now made room for a wood-heated sauna in the adjoining trees.

"Our place sleeps eight and was designed with the thought of the place being full with visitors and our family. Even with a full house, the open concept allows everyone to be together," notes Peter. "We can be cooking while others read or play board games."

Brian Coulter was the project manager for the cabin build and has since become a good friend of the Moffets. The raising of the timber frame with help of a crane reaching over the trees "was pretty much bang on," according to Brian. He adds, "Certainly for me I like the fact that all the wood was sourced locally. Beyond the building process, I think that Peter and Linda have made such a beautiful and unique cabin, and that they opened it to people within the community of Rossland, friends, and friends of friends is one of the things that makes it all so special."

OPPOSITE Fir slabs float on stringers to retain an open feeling at the stair. Southwest light filters through the forest into the stairwell.

Bents and Bays

The construction language of timber framing relies heavily on *bents*, which are lines of assembled timbers running perpendicular to the gable ridge. The bent determines the shape of the cabin, fixing its height and width. It takes two bent lines to form a bay, so the Moffet cabin has three bays (at 10 ft./ 14 ft./10 ft.) in between four bent lines. Not all bays need to be the same width, and collectively they determine the length of a cabin.

Spanning between bents are beams, girts, and purlins. Girts span horizontally between posts and beams, making up the floor structure. Purlins span between rafter members of the bent and help hold up the roof. These terms, along with pegs, tenons, bird's mouths, queen posts, collar beams, and struts, make up the rich language of timber framing.

This serene cabin presents its porch first to suggest the rich outdoor life experienced by its owners. The front stoop greets guests but is also a place to sit and observe the warm glow of sunsets.

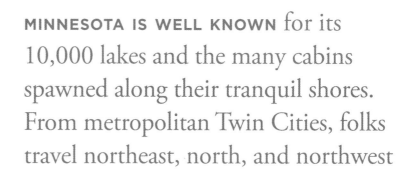

MINNESOTA IS WELL KNOWN for its 10,000 lakes and the many cabins spawned along their tranquil shores. From metropolitan Twin Cities, folks travel northeast, north, and northwest

Trout Fishing in Minnesota

to reach their lakeside retreat, clogging highways and freeways every holiday and summer weekend. Dave and Beth chose an alternate course, driving southeast into the hill and stream country of the Mississippi River Valley. Only an hour and a half from their home, they found an abundance of wildlife and the tranquility they seek away from urban life.

Dave and Beth purchased 87 acres, land that makes poor farmland but

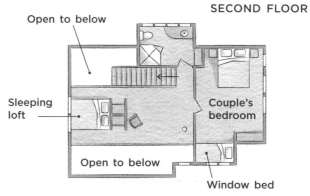

ABOVE The kitchen is central to the main level, a convenient serving place to dining room, porch, and terrace. The cabinets were made from local hardwoods.

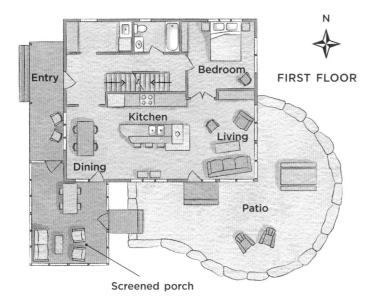

N

FIRST FLOOR

Entry

Bedroom

Kitchen

Living

Dining

Patio

Screened porch

SECOND FLOOR

Open to below

Sleeping loft

Couple's bedroom

Open to below

Window bed

constitutes a rich ecosystem. The land is characterized as a broad coulee (or valley), with a trout stream meandering through it. The coulee walls are composed of limestone ledges rising 50 ft. to 70 ft. to the agrarian prairie above. To reach most of the meadows on the property, you have to ford the stream in several places.

Why did they choose this spot? According to Beth, "The natural landscape is what we find most appealing. We love the sounds of water rippling over the rocks in the river, and we love the wildlife that inhabits our land. The rock walls that follow along the river's edge make for incredible sounds during a thunderstorm, with the thunder echoing off the walls."

You enter the property at its western edge where an old farmstead once stood. Dave and Beth hired me to design a cabin for them, and collectively we decided that the old farmhouse site had been a good choice for the farmer and was an excellent choice for them. It provided good solar access, a fine view across the meadows, protection against the cold northwest winds from a grove of pine trees, and high ground in case of potential stream flooding.

The cabin is aligned from east to west, providing extensive southern solar exposure. The entry, screened porch, and dining

ABOVE The sleeping loft features a two-sided open closet and a full-size bed with a sunset window view beyond.

LEFT Cottage-style double-hung windows have a large lower sash for better viewing from an armchair. The slate floor is heated and easy to maintain.

113

ABOVE The couple's bedroom on the second floor has an open closet and an additional sleeping or reading niche.

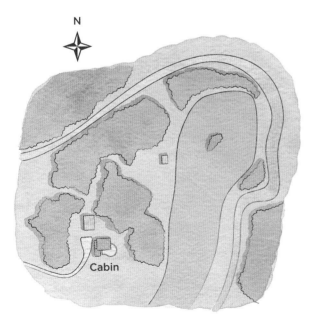

N

Cabin

area are to the west and living space to the east with a view to a bend in the river. In the middle is the kitchen and a heat-storage stove (see the sidebar on the facing page), with utilities, a bathroom, and a bedroom to the north.

Dave and Beth's bedroom is upstairs, tucked under the roof with an eastern view over the stream and meadows. It features open clothes storage and a window bed for curling up with a good book. Also on this level is a bathroom and sleeping loft. The loft bed is built in, with clothes storage at the head and a western viewing window at the foot, and is accessed independently from opposite sides, a little like Thomas Jefferson's bed at Monticello.

One of the cabin's defining features is the profusion of wood on the interior, much of it acquired from local mills. The ceilings and walls are birch and pine, the stairs are maple, and the dining table is walnut. Interior doors and built-in cabinets were sourced locally. Fir beams hold up the loft. "We like the charm and smallness of our space," says Beth, "and the open beam structure is somewhat raw and artsy at the same time."

In just a few years of use, Dave and Beth have come to enjoy their cabin in all seasons. Spring finds them trout fishing and turkey hunting and also tracking the migratory birds heading north. Summer brings trail hiking and biking and a cool dip in the river. Autumn heralds a spectacle of color, bonfires in the fire pit, and serious stargazing into the clear night sky. Winter is for tobogganing, snowshoeing, and splitting firewood.

"Once we arrive, we turn up the floor heat, stoke up the stove, and then head out for a brisk walk around the property," says Beth. They might check to see if their resident bald eagles are perched above their nest, or listen for the call of the barn owl. "We love our cabin and we love the setting," notes Beth. "The beauty, peace, and quiet down in the valley never get old."

The southeastern terrace is protected from cool northwest winds by the cabin and the tree buffer that remains from the homestead that once stood on this spot.

Soapstone Heater

The heat-retaining fireplace in Dave and Beth's kitchen is made from soapstone quarried and fabricated in Finland. It arrived at their site as soapstone precut blocks and was assembled on location by certified installers.

This unit burns wood very efficiently and may require firing only every 12 hours or so. Soapstone holds the heat, radiating to adjacent space slowly over time. Unlike a metal woodstove, it is not red hot to the touch, so it is particularly safe for children and thus can be located central to a room for radiant heat distribution.

Soapstone heaters are available in many different sizes, configurations, and aesthetic characters. Some include a baking oven. Because they are made of stone, they require foundation support.

Bathed in filtered sunshine, this modest weekend cabin nestles in the woods. Isolated from neighbors, the site promotes solitude, interrupted only by the sound of rustling leaves.

THE TRIANGLE AREA OF North Carolina is a vibrant metropolis driven by the youthful energy of its many universities, research centers, and an international airport that are the core of its existence. But for one faculty member at North Carolina State, an equally strong drive is

Escape to Boone Mountain

the need to escape that energy for the peace and solitude of Boone Mountain, three hours to the west. Here, summer hiking, winter snowboarding, or stargazing under a night sky serve to reconnect him and his family with nature and with each other.

Architecture professor Thomas Barrie and his wife, Lisa, bought 6 acres of mountainside as a place where they and their two sons could unwind. Thomas designed a modest cabin for the family, with an 800-sq.-ft. footprint and a 250-sq.-ft. loft.

Access to the wooded site is from above and from the west. Thomas's design cascades down to the entry and then

BELOW The bath is wrapped in smooth masonry blocks and local cypress. Showering occurs outside.

Carolina that has no air conditioning." He also thought the warm wood could better express the craft of its making.

The cabin is not without color, as a vibrant yellow highlights the kitchen and a brilliant red announces the upper stair wall. "I led the interior design process to select furniture, paint colors, bedding, and kitchenware," says Lisa. "And I rejoice each time I enter the house."

The cabin and its contents reflect a strong desire that Thomas and Lisa share for a more refined, less cluttered existence in their mountain retreat. They purposely created less room for storage so they wouldn't collect unnecessary items. "Less is more in Boone," explains Lisa.

Routines are beginning to set in at the cabin, not the least of which is cooking the great produce available at the local farmers' market. They've hosted many friends and enjoy sharing their experiences with others. Thomas likes waking with Lisa at sunrise in their east-facing bedroom, before they move to the loft overlooking the woods for their morning yoga session.

Lisa reflects back to the early days of planning the cabin: "I certainly remember strolling the property with Thomas and the boys and marking the site with string and wooden stakes." She wondered if such a small footprint could accommodate all of their needs. "But it exceeded our expectations in every possible way. We often look back to the process of building the cabin as such a labor of love and vision. We made it through and are so much the better because of it."

THE TRIANGLE AREA OF North Carolina is a vibrant metropolis driven by the youthful energy of its many universities, research centers, and an international airport that are the core of its existence. But for one faculty member at North Carolina State, an equally strong drive is

Escape to Boone Mountain

the need to escape that energy for the peace and solitude of Boone Mountain, three hours to the west. Here, summer hiking, winter snowboarding, or stargazing under a night sky serve to reconnect him and his family with nature and with each other.

Architecture professor Thomas Barrie and his wife, Lisa, bought 6 acres of mountainside as a place where they and their two sons could unwind. Thomas designed a modest cabin for the family, with an 800-sq.-ft. footprint and a 250-sq.-ft. loft.

Access to the wooded site is from above and from the west. Thomas's design cascades down to the entry and then

A lofty living room drops three steps down from the entry and is surrounded by views into the woods. The heated floor is polished concrete. Primary colors of yellow cabinets and red chairs enrich the space.

LEFT The horizontal lines of the cabin mimic the earth's strata, from which the stair cascades down.

steps down again within the living room. An outdoor terrace is open to the southeast and is framed by living and bedroom spaces. The whole design approach is an interesting juxtaposition of space and movement that aligns on the cardinal directions.

The main two-story volume is an east/west shed with its roof rising to southern sunshine. The roof overhang is set to block out high summer sun but capture the passive solar gain of low-angled winter sun. Unique to the cabin is a small Zen perch off the loft that has views north and west and back toward the entry path.

Thomas designed the whole project on a 4-ft. grid module, both vertically and horizontally. The two-story portion of the main living space is 12 ft. wide by 36 ft. long and 20 ft. tall. The living room expands to 16 ft. by 16 ft. The bedroom wing is 12 ft. by 16 ft. and the entry 8 ft. by 8 ft. The second-level Zen perch measures 4 ft. by 4 ft. Even outdoor spaces are modules of 4 ft., with an 8-ft. by 8-ft. outdoor shower and a 12-ft. by 12-ft. patio.

The cabin is sheathed inside and out in local cypress. "It's sustainable," says Tom. "It's also mildew and mold resistant, which is an important consideration in a house in North

FIRST FLOOR

SECOND FLOOR

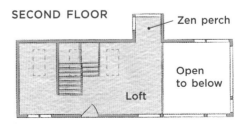

Carolina that has no air conditioning." He also thought the warm wood could better express the craft of its making.

The cabin is not without color, as a vibrant yellow highlights the kitchen and a brilliant red announces the upper stair wall. "I led the interior design process to select furniture, paint colors, bedding, and kitchenware," says Lisa. "And I rejoice each time I enter the house."

The cabin and its contents reflect a strong desire that Thomas and Lisa share for a more refined, less cluttered existence in their mountain retreat. They purposely created less room for storage so they wouldn't collect unnecessary items. "Less is more in Boone," explains Lisa.

Routines are beginning to set in at the cabin, not the least of which is cooking the great produce available at the local farmers' market. They've hosted many friends and enjoy sharing their experiences with others. Thomas likes waking with Lisa at sunrise in their east-facing bedroom, before they move to the loft overlooking the woods for their morning yoga session.

Lisa reflects back to the early days of planning the cabin: "I certainly remember strolling the property with Thomas and the boys and marking the site with string and wooden stakes." She wondered if such a small footprint could accommodate all of their needs. "But it exceeded our expectations in every possible way. We often look back to the process of building the cabin as such a labor of love and vision. We made it through and are so much the better because of it."

Designing on a 4-Ft. Grid

A North American standard for building materials is 4 ft. x 8 ft., with plywood, oriented strand board, and gypsum board all fabricated in that size. Linear board materials often are available in 8-ft., 12-ft., and 16-ft. lengths. Concrete blocks, another material in Thomas's palette, are 8 in. x 16 in. (with grout), which are factors of 4 ft.

Designing from the basis of a grid can regulate sizing decisions for all rooms. Frank Lloyd Wright laid out his Usonian houses on a 2-ft. by 4-ft. grid, marked both on the drawings and on the actual concrete floor.

Thomas's 4-ft. grid is applied, somewhat uniquely, both horizontally and vertically. In addition to its implication on the exterior, it also informs interior details such as the cypress joints, concrete floor expansion cuts, and the patio pavers.

Afternoon sunlight filters into the living/dining space. The cypress paneling lightens the room.

The screened porch at the western end of this sleek Canadian family cabin is overlaid with a cedar-lath privacy grille.

FROM TENT TO YURT to cabin—such was the shelter progression made by two busy Canadian physicians, Pauline and Howie, looking for respite from their demanding careers. Stealing away time

Stealth Cabin

for pilgrimages into the wilderness was hard to schedule, so they needed their own property where an advance reservation wasn't necessary. They also wanted a place that was easy to get to, ideally within a two-hour drive of Toronto.

They found the property they desired in 2006, a large parcel of forest with 1,300 ft. of shorefront on a motor-restricted lake. There was a provincial park adjacent and a 40-cottage limit on the lake. Keen hikers and campers, they set about exploring their land in

ABOVE A table of reclaimed barn wood awaits victuals from the efficient galley kitchen.

search of a permanent campsite. A tent platform served them well for a couple of years, until growing concern for bears and a desire for a better cookstove encouraged them to move up to a yurt by 2009. A leaky roof after a heavy snowfall helped Pauline come to the realization that a more permanent cabin was called for.

But now came the quandary. Howie pictured a rustic log structure, primitive with an outhouse out back. Pauline was thinking more along the lines of modern, light filled, with 21st-century conveniences. Pauline's familiarity with the architectural firm Superkül suggested they tap the firm's skill at negotiating disparate goals. Partners Meg Graham and Andre D'Elia, a couple themselves, had regularly worked with couples on projects where spouses have opposing visions.

Howie appreciated the firm's commitment to sustainability and durability and their proclivity for blending structures into natural settings. He was further swayed by their suggestion that a modern form could still be wrapped in wood, inside and out, and have the warmth and simplicity he was looking for.

Meg and Andre's solution is a 1,500-sq.-ft., three-bedroom, two-bath, single-level cabin. The plan separates entry and guest

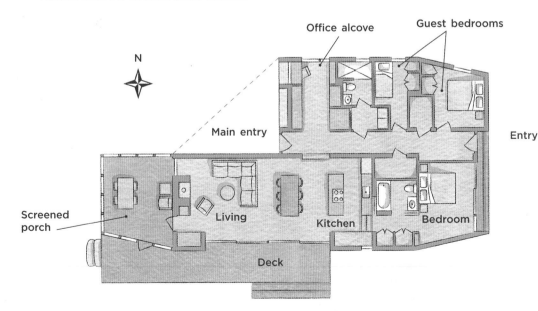

OPPOSITE The dining/living room, which features a high-efficiency wood-burning fireplace with a concrete surround, has a filtered southern view to the lake. The polished concrete floor is radiant-heated.

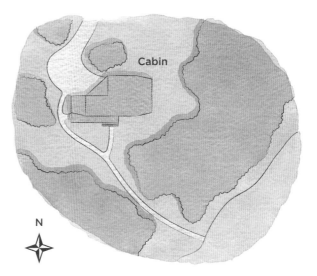

Cabin

N

ABOVE The main entry is sheltered by a triangular canopy with a cedar soffit; the bay to the left of the door is used for outdoor storage of firewood.

ABOVE The cedar grille work screens the driveway and helps protect the porch from cool westerly winds.

FAR RIGHT A snug bunkroom awaits family and friends in the guest wing. The painted beds are a complementary contrast to the cedar paneling.

RIGHT Pauline and Howie both enjoy their book nook with its south-facing window overlooking the lake.

The horizontal cedar strips that surround the screened porch and the deck fascia contrast with the vertical tree trunks of the surrounding pine forest.

quarters from living space. Thus, in winter use, only their wing needs to be heated. The elongated plan has "chamfered," or tapered, ends, which visually reduce the cabin's scale in the forest setting and gave rise to its "Stealth Cabin" moniker.

The main entry to the cabin is from the northwest under a triangular canopy, which also doubles as outdoor storage for firewood. The main living space orients to the south for passive solar gain in winter months. A modest roof overhang over the south-facing windows and the decision to preserve close-by deciduous trees serve to protect the glass from excessive summer heat. A screened porch at the west end is partially clad in wood slats for additional privacy and wind protection.

Howie likes that the design has a few intimate niches, one where he can get away for office work and another adjacent to the kitchen where he can curl up with a good book while watching Pauline prep for a meal. He has also been known to take a nap there.

Pauline and Howie have juggled their schedules so they can spend more time at the cabin. Christmas is a stay of 10 days, and they are in residence in the forest for a full month in the summer. Shorter stays are peppered throughout the year, and activities now include sailboating in the summer, mountain biking in spring and fall, and snowshoeing and cross-country skiing in the winter. "We love being outside," notes Pauline, "and inside it feels like we are still living outside."

All in a Name

Pauline and Howie's cabin is nicknamed "Stealth Cabin," although in this province in Canada it might equally be referred to as their *cottage.* Should it be relocated 400 miles southeast into the Adirondacks, it might carry the term *camp.* Cabin, cottage, and camp are interchangeable terms and are derivative more of the cultural base of the announcer than of the style of the building.

The *Stealth* part of the name is a nod to the building's appearance in both shape and materiality: As the exterior photos show, the cabin does look a lot like the fuselage of a stealth bomber. Names for more traditional cabins might derive from known cabin types, such as "A-Frame" or "Greenway Gables."

Naming a cabin can be a fun family endeavor, although not all names will last across generations. Nurturing a name with a sign at the driveway, on cabin stationery, or inscribed on the cover of a guest book may help to enhance longevity.

An ensemble of shed roofs lifts to the tree canopies, as multiple small structures come together to weave their way through the trees.

MAINE ARCHITECT Will Winkelman explains that it's a great start to the design process when clients really know their property. That was the case with this island project on a small lake in central

A Maine Island Camp

Maine for two Portland attorneys. One of them had attended a camp on the same lake in his youth, and the other had enjoyed a similar camp lake experience elsewhere. After buying the land, the couple built a tent platform and camped there with their two children for several summers. As the years passed, they began to understand the diurnal and seasonal changes the property goes through, and they came

to appreciate the value of the sheltering canopy of pines and oaks that covered the island.

In early meetings with Will and his associate, Melissa Andrews, the couple expressed concern for saving trees and building a cabin that would blend in with the surroundings. They would be removing a modest existing cabin on the island and utilizing its clearing 60 ft. from the water for the site of their new structure. Its location on the southern point of the three-acre island would allow them to capture sweeping panoramic views.

Will and Melissa's design idea for the cabin was to break the structure down into three separate parts (or "pods"), with connected porch links so they could more easily weave the building through the trees. Zoning rules required them to keep the cabin to a maximum footprint of 1,500 sq. ft. and a height limit of 20 ft. They explored alternative roof schemes, comparing vernacular gables versus more contemporary sheds and flat roofs on the porches (see the sidebar on the facing page).

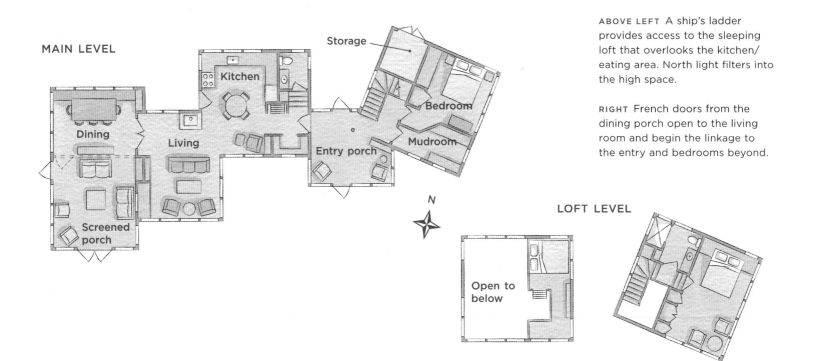

MAIN LEVEL

Storage

Kitchen

Bedroom

Dining

Living

Mudroom

Entry porch

Screened porch

N

LOFT LEVEL

Open to below

ABOVE LEFT A ship's ladder provides access to the sleeping loft that overlooks the kitchen/eating area. North light filters into the high space.

RIGHT French doors from the dining porch open to the living room and begin the linkage to the entry and bedrooms beyond.

Design Options

Architects typically begin the design process after a thorough site analysis and upon gleaning the owners' goals, aspirations, and budget. Many architects then present alternative solutions to the owners as a way to further understand how their clients make decisions and how they respond to aesthetics.

Will Winkelman and his associate, Melissa Andrews, developed two schemes for their island clients, with similar plans but with different roof forms. Melissa's sketches highlighted the difference between an assembly of gable forms versus a series of sheds. The owners immediately opted for the shed-roof scheme, preferring its outward thrust to the understory of the pine trees and the way it would filter light deep into each space.

A one-and-a-half-story pod flanks the east end of the camp and deftly contains two levels of sleeping within its 20-ft. height. This pod is joined by an entry porch to the kitchen/dining/living pod. The high ceiling in the kitchen lifts to an open sleeping loft, which is reached by a ship's ladder. At the west end, a summer living porch offers broad views to the water. Folded glass panels can be used to close off half the porch on cooler days.

Building on the island was a challenge because all materials and laborers had to be transported there by boat. Builder Henry Banks fabricated his own unique barge for the occasion. As winter set in and ice formed, Henry's crewmembers were able to walk to the island pulling sleds. With thicker ice, snowmobiles and eventually pick-up trucks could be used.

A few oak trees had to be cut down to make room for the camp and the solar shed nearby. The felled trees were milled on site with a portable sawmill for later use as interior finishes and furniture. Henry was also able to use his local connections to reclaim some Southern yellow pine from a Maine paper

TOP Morning light filters into the east wing second-level bedroom.

ABOVE The lower bedroom in the east wing has a supply of puzzles and bedside reading.

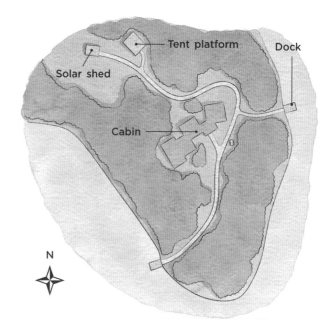

The dining area of the screened porch can be closed with windows that drop on the west wall and accordion over on the north wall.

ABOVE The loft bedroom has built-in storage created with reclaimed heart pine from a dismantled Maine paper mill.

RIGHT Because the cabin is on a small island, workmen and construction materials all had to arrive by boat from a mainland dock.

ABOVE The living room has a corner exposure to the lake and is warmed by the soapstone-clad woodstove.

RIGHT A stair with fir treads leads down from the upper bedroom in the east wing of the cabin.

mill. "It was the best load of wood I had ever purchased," Henry is said to have exclaimed. This cache was milled to size for exposed roof-framing members and some of the woodwork. The exterior is clad in hand-split cedar shakes, which have a textural quality similar to the surrounding tree bark. A charcoal gray penetrating stain helped achieve a similar color to the bark.

Solar panels mounted atop a shed on higher ground north of the camp generate the modest amount of energy needed. Propane is used as backup to fire a generator and for cooking. Although the camp was begun as a seasonal structure, the owners have winterized the center living pod and can cocoon there for short winter stays.

The owner is full of praise for the amazing team of designers and builders of his camp. "It's the most incredible craftsmanship, just like a fine piece of furniture," he states. "The design is understated, simple, and dramatically uplifting. It's photogenic, but living in it is even better than the photographs."

Nestled Together

A trout stream flows down from the Teton Mountains past this family encampment of new and refurbished cabins.

CHILDHOOD MEMORIES RUN DEEP in our psyche and sometimes surface later in life to inform cabin decisions. Kelly's roots were in Montana, the big sky and mountain country most of us read

Fish Creek Cabins

about or see on TV westerns. Kelly left the wide-open spaces for college, met Curtis, married, and settled in Houston, Texas. Children arrived and soon the family was escaping the Texas heat to the closest mountains Kelly could find, the Colorado Rockies.

Curtis wanted to be near water and after their adult daughter moved to Jackson Hole, Wyoming, Kelly began looking for fly-fishing cabins near the majestic Teton Mountains where

ALPHA CABIN

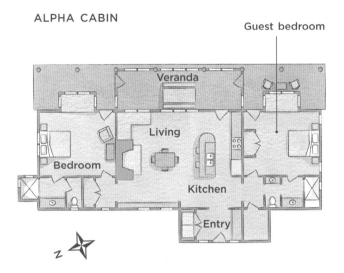

Guest bedroom

Veranda

Living

Bedroom

Kitchen

Entry

they could build a family lodge. The property she found is on Fish Creek and had a ranch house that was only worthy of demolition. She also was introduced to the Ankeny clan, Papa Charlie and his son Jake, both capable of demo or new construction, and daughters-in-law Shawn, an architect, and Dana, a property manager.

As the demo crew dug in, finding historical treasures such as a buried-car septic system, Kelly and Shawn had time to envision a future for the property. An old log cabin close to the creek was deemed worthy of restoration, and the idea of a large family lodge was quickly nixed in favor of a more humble approach. A new, smaller two-bedroom cabin was envisioned on the ranch house site and a second historic cabin was purchased for an adjacent spot downstream. This would give them an encampment of three retreat structures that could be enjoyed in diverse ways to fit many combinations of family and friends.

RIGHT A glazed porch nestled between two open porches overlooks the trout stream. Wood paneling, nostalgic light fixtures, and a wooden picnic table maintain a simple rustic character.

Log Cabin Preservation

Log cabins have a mystique and charm that often encourage their preservation, usually at their original site but occasionally miles away at a new location. Logs can be marked, dismantled, and reassembled. A rotted sill log can be replaced or an additional log added to create a taller interior space. A window can be cut larger or a door taller. Log structures do have constraints such as retaining their corners and having sufficient header logs over doors and windows to carry roof loads.

Architect Shawn Ankeny notes that repurposing log structures is open to tough interpretations by local building code officials as to both structural adequacies and energy performance. Roofs can receive added structure and insulation from above, allowing them to retain the historic interior ceiling character.

Builder Jake Ankeny inserted a new floor system in the historic Fish Creek cabins that also facilitated running new plumbing and electrical distributions. A few logs were replaced or repaired and new chinking was added throughout. The pine logs were cob-blasted to remove old paint and varnishes, and a fresh coat of Transformation Stain was applied to the exterior. Although the foundations weren't great, the building crew was able to shore them up without needing to lift the old log structure.

N

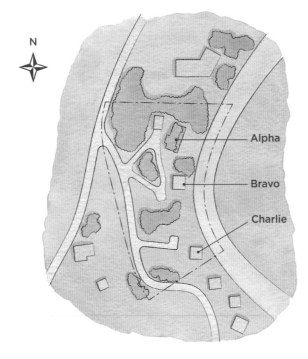

Alpha

Bravo

Charlie

ABOVE The compact living space in Bravo cabin looks back toward the main Alpha cabin.

LEFT The corner bedroom in Bravo cabin is in close proximity to the creek, its existing location grandfathered in since it was only remodeled.

Shawn's plan for the new main cabin, which they named Alpha, has living space sandwiched between two bedroom/bath suites. A veranda stretches across the creek side of the cabin, and each bedroom includes a cushioned bay window large enough for additional sleeping or just curling up with a good book while listening to the fast-flowing stream.

The two historic log cabins, Bravo and Charlie, were renovated to include living space, bathroom, bedroom, and bunkroom. Both offer the opportunity of fly fishing right outside the door and with Alpha share a fire pit for cookouts and sing-alongs.

Kelly, a self-taught decorator, furnished each cabin with hardware, light fixtures, and artwork that retain a rustic west-

ABOVE Each of the two bedrooms in the Alpha cabin has a comfortable window seat alcove for book reading or a sleeping child.

LEFT A historical marker attests to the origins of this settlement and the beginnings of homesteading in the Jackson Hole Valley.

ern aesthetic. In the new cabin, drywall was eschewed in favor of pine paneling installed vertically and horizontally. The fireplace is clad in a regional moss rock that enhances the interior's timeless character.

The family greatly enjoys their stays at the encampment along the creek, whether for summer fly fishing, rafting, mountain biking, or winter skiing. The site is also home to "The Children's Grand Adventure," a joint program of the Teton Science School and the Texas Children Center in Houston. Youth whose lives are defined by the grueling physical and psychological demands of cancer can enjoy a welcome respite among rushing water, bird songs at sunrise, and shooting stars over bonfires.

With lights aglow in the early evening, the Alpha cabin is an enticing beacon from across the meadow on the other side of the creek. The foothills to the Teton Mountains rise in the background.

Six decades of family memories are recorded in the artifacts on display above the granite and brick fireplace, each with a story to be told on a chilly evening.

"THANK YOU, DAD, for your foresight. Stepping off the 'Fetch-n-Carry' onto our dock, I take off my watch and switch to Mountainy time. I hear the wind sigh in the pines and the lap of the waves on the rocky lakeshore. I am happy in my soul at that moment."

The Luxury of Place

So reflects Greta Nettleton as she embarks on another summer sojourn at the family camp in Maine. Alone or with her sister Sarah or with her husband, Rex, and sons, Alexander and Luc, she'll make her way along with her provisions to the simple structure that has been the summer home to her family since 1958. That is when her father, John, bought Hemlock Lodge from the widow Leila Miller.

The development at Mountainy Pond began back in 1926 when a man called Hinckley purchased a large land-holding and started selling lots. By the time of the financial crash of 1929, only 13 lots had been sold, all located along the eastern shore with sunset views. Following the crash, the camp owners collectively bought the remaining land

ABOVE A filter of trees between the main cabin and the lake protects the shoreline from the appearance of development.

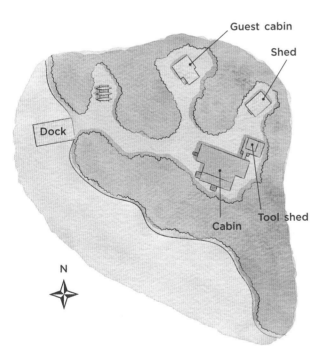

Guest cabin

Shed

Dock

Cabin

Tool shed

N

and established the Mountainy Pond Club with a common goal of nature preservation and solitude. No motorized boats except for the collective "Fetch-n-Carry," no electricity, and no roads were rules then and they're still adhered to today.

All the structures at the encampment are off-grid, so it means that learning to cook in and on a woodstove or heating your shower water from a solar tank is the norm. Cell phones are useful only after hiking up one of the surrounding hills, and they may have to be charged using a solar cell. Gas-powered refrigeration is limited, so it's best to bring provisions that don't need to be kept cold. It does begin to feel a lot like camping—though you don't have to bring the tent.

Life at the camp takes on the diurnal swing of the day: up at dawn for a refreshing swim and in bed after sunset for quiet reading by flashlight, candles, or gas lamps. The solitude is interrupted only by the laughter and banter of fellow residents, the occasional birdcall, and the brief run of the gasoline-powered pump hoisting lake water to the attic storage tanks for indoor plumbing.

Blueberry Pancakes

According to Sarah Nettleton, "Cooking on a woodstove is a skill set passed down through the family, starting with splitting the kindling and stove wood. Filling the wood box with slow-burning hardwoods and fast-burning spruce and then tuning the fire is the start to pancakes the next morning. While the stove is heating up, 40 minutes or so (the cook gets up early), the nephews paddle over to the island to pick blueberries for blueberry pancakes. All this 'studied inconvenience' is the pleasure of this place. The stove has a nickel plate on it identifying it as made in Bangor by the Wood and Bishop Company."

ABOVE The family dock is not just for freshwater diving and canoe launching but also serves as an extension of cabin living . . . and a place to greet neighbors boating by.

LEFT All is within plain sight in the open kitchen, making it easy to find the utensils needed for prepping dinner.

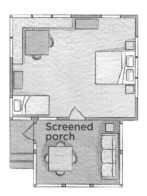

Bedrooms

Bedroom

Dining **Kitchen**

Living room

MAIN CABIN

Tool shed

Screened porch

GUEST CABIN

Sleeping near an open window in the guest cabin means awaking to songbirds and the splash of cabinmates taking an early-morning swim.

The Nettleton Camp contains four structures: the original three-bedroom cabin, a linked utility shed, a guest cabin designed by sister Sarah (an architect), and a freestanding shed. Except on cool days, much of daily life occurs on either the open porch of the main cabin, the screened porch at the guest cabin, or a few steps away at the dock. The evening meal is just the opposite of fast food, with a lot of thought going into the best preparation of the blueberry harvest or mushroom gathering.

The interior of the main cabin is exposed studs and fir plank sheathing. The fireplace and mantel are original local granite and brick. The structure had been mothballed for many years before John bought it. He transformed a porch into a bedroom and subdivided another bedroom to turn it into a powder room and a small sleeping space.

Greta concludes that "Dad's phrase, 'studied inconvenience' sums up Mountainy's relationship to the hectic pace of modern life. The bowl of hills surrounding the lake hides all view and sound of the outside world. We have the freedom to live simply and to accomplish small tasks with patience and satisfaction. We can enjoy the company of many old friends around the lake spontaneously and informally."

The candle
lanterns
are lit for a
late-summer
dinner on
the well-used
open porch.

The communal dining hall and guest bunkroom building is surrounded
by the native vegetation of the hill country of central Texas.

IN OUR MOBILE AMERICAN culture, it's increasingly common to live in cities far away from extended family and roots, and in those situations, long-term friendships are often nurtured

Shared Compound

with folks who are not relatives. In Austin, Texas, just such a group of close friends had fantasized about buying a fleet of Airstreams® in retirement and parking them on collective land in a pastoral landscape. While visiting mutual friends west of Austin on the Llano River, they heard that a nearby parcel of land was for sale. The river is known for fly fishing and for its scenic sandstone bluffs. It seemed that dreams of trail biking,

The Art of Sharing

Jodi notes that sharing is made easier when all parties have a long history of developing common values. They understand their respectful idiosyncrasies and know what buttons not to push. They share similar activities and yet have their private space to retreat to.

The four couples do indeed have some informal rules, such as changing the sheets when you leave, washing the towels, and cleaning up the kitchen. They have been pretty amazed at their collective success. And they have partnership agreements that account for any potential departures.

"We had a great party here last Christmas, of everyone with children and friends. There were people sleeping everywhere, maybe 25 in all. We cooked, ate, drank, and sang songs at the bonfire. These are the people I love."

RIGHT In each of the four cabins, a divider screen is provided for sleeping privacy. The interior is pine plywood walls and a polished concrete floor.

hunting, river rafting, and great cookouts might finally be realized.

Jodi Zipp and her husband, Fred, along with three other couples were skeptical when they first saw the property. Invasive grasses and privet shrubs were threatening the mature oaks. A previous owner had carelessly carved a road down to the river, leaving piles of debris along the way. However, one of the friends, an urban planner, could see beyond the mess to the opportunity for their shared oasis. A quick purchase and plenty of sweat equity in debris clearing and the "Llano Exit Strategy," or the "LES" as it is known, was born.

The mystique of Airstreams quickly gave way to a desire for more permanent structures, and Austin architect Matt Garcia was hired to visualize a solution. The four couples were looking for something utilitarian, easy to maintain, and supportive of their communal spirit. They wanted to be environmentally sensitive and make wise use of local builders and materials.

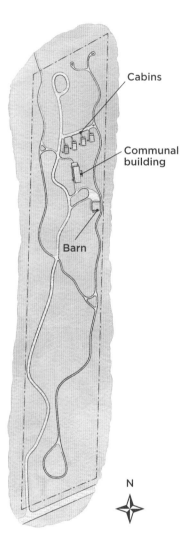

LEFT The community of four couples comes together in the communal cooking and dining hall.

Cabins

Communal building

Barn

N

Metal Sheds

Utilitarian metal pole barns are as American as apple pie and can be found across the nation. Although most are commonly used for agrarian purposes, they can take on a wide variety of functions from horse barns, auto-maintenance garages, fast-food joints, and even churches. They are a primitive and basic form of shelter from the elements.

At the LES, metal sheds represent the casual nature of the gathering of friends where pretensions, if they had existed, were jettisoned when leaving the Austin city limits. The sheds are a manifestation of that old cabin axiom, "It's just a shell to hold memories of a life."

A butterfly roof on the communal building collects rainfall for landscape irrigation. Each of the private cabins also has a tank for water storage.

CABIN

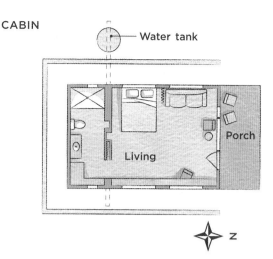

Matt created a compound of four individual private cabins, one shared communal structure, and a storage barn. The cabins are modest, just 350 sq. ft., containing a bed, a few soft chairs, and a bathroom. They are individually assigned to each couple but can be used by others when not occupied by the owner.

The communal building has a spacious kitchen with industrial stove, dual dishwashers, and an oversized refrigerator. A granite-covered island separates the kitchen from the dining area for a large gathering of family and friends. It also has a deck with a big picnic table. A guest bunkroom and bath were also added to the communal building.

The exteriors of all the buildings are clad in corrugated galvanized steel reminiscent of rural Texas farm buildings. Butterfly shed roofs are designed to collect irrigation water to benefit plant growth in this arid climate. Large expansive glass is on the north side, with roof overhangs to protect from overhead summer sun. The structures are well insulated and heated and cooled by a heat pump.

Interiors are simply sheathed in pine plywood, which is used both on walls and for shelving. Bathroom towel rods, toilet paper holders, and bathrobe hooks are made from standard pipe fittings. Concrete floors are left natural to give an industrial chic aesthetic.

ABOVE The four private cabins have high windows on neighboring walls and large north-viewing windows.

A neighborhood of similar, yet not identical, three-level cabins dots a hillside overlooking a stream in the Village of Cheshire, North Carolina.

WHEN PEOPLE SEEK A place of refuge from an active urban life, we generally assume that what they want is a cabin in the forest, along a river, or at a lakeshore. Not for Lisa and Jon, who went looking for a getaway place to escape the summer heat of New Orleans. Sure, they longed for the

Tree House

coolness of nature, but they also craved the convenience of a coffee shop, a few groceries, and a restaurant. They found all of that and more in the new community of The Village of Cheshire near picturesque Black Mountain, North Carolina.

Planned as a peaceful hamlet, The Village of Cheshire is a collection of homes, "tree houses," and cabins nestled into the North Carolina hills. There's also a village center a short walk across the village green, complete with retail shops, a fresh market, and plenty of options for dining. Porches overlook Camp Branch Creek, while native rhododendron and mountain laurel give fragrance and color to nearby hiking trails.

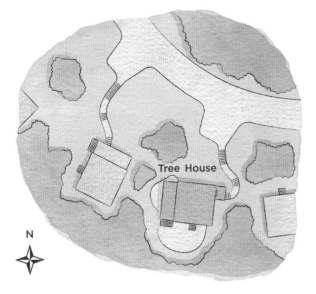

N

Tree House

Lisa and Jon purchased a Tree House home designed by Asheville architect Michael McDonough. In an effort to preserve trees and a hillside, the three-story houses were limited by village covenants to a footprint of 500 sq. ft.—a size, as Michael notes, that's comparable to a modest two-car garage. The challenge of designing a smart vertical house with environmental sensitivity would be a test of his ingenuity.

A typical horizontal home establishes rooms linked by hallways, but in a tight vertical house, the stairway is the unifying element. Michael placed bedrooms on top and bottom levels, with kitchen, living, and dining on the middle level. The stairways are left open to each bedroom to visually increase their size, and privacy is created by the middle living space.

By tucking the house into the hillside, it was possible to place the mid-level entry at the stair landing, while ample light and a walkout patio enhance the lowest level. Farther up the hill, a landscaped terrace can be reached from the living room level and attached porch. The small home is made to feel larger by these outdoor living spaces.

Stacking bathroom, kitchen, and laundry water pipes into a vertical wet core creates greater efficiency. Air ducts are limited to the core and are thus kept out of the main floor ceiling, which meant that an exposed beam and decking floor system could be employed to give the appearance of added height to the room. (Beam and decking floor systems easily transmit

LEFT The upper-level bedroom is open to the stairway, creating a larger and more light-filled spatial experience.

OPPOSITE The main (middle) level is living/dining/kitchen space accessed from the entry a half level below.

The Village of Cheshire Tree Houses

The Village of Cheshire is informed by a relatively new urbanist planning concept known as traditional neighborhood development (TND), whereby great ideas in town design are drawn from successful villages in the Carolinas and England. Key attributes include quaint narrow streets, preserved and enhanced vegetation, diverse and densely spaced housing, a village green, and a small-shop commercial center. Its setting is in a forested valley with views to High Top Mountain.

Originally developed by the architectural firm of Andres Duany and Elizabeth Plater-Zyberk, the Cheshire master plan created sites for more than a dozen Tree Houses, 10 of which have been built to date. The original footprint limit of 500 sq. ft. was eased only slightly to 24 ft. x 24 ft. in later units (plus an attached outdoor porch). New design iterations within that limit have been created by a number of designers. In addition to "Winnie Place," as the Lisa and Jon's Tree House is known, Michael McDonough has designed three other unique Tree Houses in the village.

LEFT Both the main and lower levels have access to outside space as porch or terraces.

BELOW Below the covered porch, a pebble-stone patio adjoins the den that doubles as a family room and guest bedroom.

MAIN LEVEL

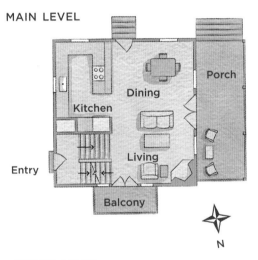

UPPER LEVEL

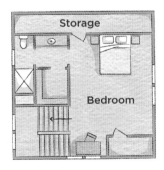

sounds, but since the bedroom above was already open to the stairwell, this wasn't an issue.)

The exterior is clad in cedar shingles with forest green trim. To add character to the simple form, brackets were used over an entry canopy and a small balcony overlooking Camp Branch Creek. The living-level porch set on timber and stone piers shelters the lower-level terrace.

In the few years they've owned it, Lisa and Jon have become totally smitten with their tree house 10 hours away from their home in New Orleans. As Lisa tells it, "When searching for a vacation home, we were attracted to the charm of Black Mountain and the funkiness of nearby Asheville. As for Cheshire Village, it was hard to beat the walking trails, pub, restaurant, and Michele's hair salon, all only a stroll away. Even our dog, Beignet, endorses the lifestyle."

ABOVE The exposed beam and decking ceiling creates a higher space without increasing the total height of the building. The TV above the fireplace is concealed behind cabinet doors when not in use.

RIGHT The main-level porch extends the modest living space of this 24-ft. x 24-ft. cabin.

A compact family cabin with seven bedrooms expands its living space with a gracious wraparound screened porch overlooking Lake Superior.

THE FIRST MEETING I HAD with the Brunkers to discuss their cabin project was with Les and Theresa, Theresa's parents, her sister and husband, along with her brother and his wife.

Full House

Eight adults all with strong opinions principally formed by the many summers they'd spent together at a particular cabin rental. Each of the siblings now had children, and the collective space needs were substantial. A budget had to be realistic, and a compact, versatile design would be necessary.

The family was quite familiar with Madeline Island, the only island of the Apostle Islands in Lake Superior that allows seasonal or yearlong homes. The parents had a sailboat moored nearby,

ABOVE A cook, a dishwasher, and four food critics can all smell the entrée in this cozy corner kitchen with its soft yellow cabinets.

which encouraged the Brunkers to purchase a buildable lot on the northwest shore of the island. The lot has a significant slope to the water and a buildable plateau and open meadow at the top, with spectacular views to the other islands and early summer sunsets.

My design for the Brunker cabin creates plenty of open space for living, dining, and the kitchen on the main level. An away room tucked behind the living room hearth is a place for games, puzzles, and quiet reading. In addition, there's room on the main level for a pantry, an entry with wood storage, a bathroom, and a bedroom. An ample screened porch extends living into the fresh air.

Up on the second level, there are four bedrooms, three with views toward Lake Superior. A one-of-a-kind family bathroom has an anteroom with three pedestal sinks at various heights, off which there are private cubicles with toilets and shower. At

MAIN FLOOR

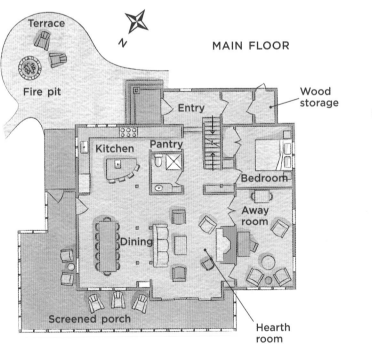

Terrace

Fire pit

Entry

Wood storage

Kitchen

Pantry

Bedroom

Away room

Dining

Hearth room

Screened porch

UPPER LEVEL

Book nook

Bedrooms

Stairs to loft

Bedrooms

ABOVE Glacially rolled fieldstone and exposed fir beams are focal points in the living room, which extends through doors to the away room.

LEFT The long dining table accommodates a dozen or more hearty eaters in this room wrapped in fir walls, ceiling, and floor.

ABOVE A book nook at the top of the second floor stairs and over the entry presents yet another potential place for sleeping.

RIGHT A unique three-sink bathroom on the second floor accommodates all family members regardless of height. Toilets and shower are in adjacent compartments. The pastel painted walls and ceiling provide a refreshing break from the many fir-paneled bedrooms.

ABOVE Bedrooms are tucked into the eaves, and ample windows create cross ventilation. Two of the bedrooms have dormer windows.

RIGHT An alternating-tread stair, a popular cabin detail, gives access to two children's lofts high under the roof ridge.

the top of the stair, a book nook with a mattress is the perfect place to curl up with a good novel or sleep another family member or friend.

The lower level has a rainy-day rumpus room (complete with a climbing wall) for rambunctious children and a space for projects, whether artistic or scientific. Also on this level is a much-needed laundry room, as well as sports equipment storage, with an external door and outdoor shower.

One of the perks of being a cabin architect is that I occasionally get to enjoy the experience of my designs by borrowing them for a weekend or longer. It's a great way to contemplate the successes and weaknesses in a design, especially with a tough critic like my wife along for the ride. In the Brunker cabin, my extended family of 16 spent a delightful four days on the island, kayaking, cooking, and just generally getting reacquainted.

Building on an Island

Living on an island has a certain romantic appeal, whereas building on an island is just a long series of headaches. This is particularly true in a cold climate where ice-in time and ice-out time are an unpredictable occurrence. Some islands have a flourishing commerce where barges arrive regularly with windows, lumber loads, hardware, and even cement trucks. Smaller lakes with few islands require a unique solution for water transport, such as buying or renting an old pontoon boat.

Island building may require designs that reflect both material limitations and a dearth of skilled craftsmen. Thin-ice conditions may constrain the building schedule to warmer months or swing months. In really cold locations where deep ice is formed, builders and materials may be transported directly to the site for a few months.

Madeline Island is served daily by ferries from Bayfield, Wisconsin, except in winter conditions or excessive wind. It is populated enough to have some builders on the island and others who make the daily ferry ride. Building materials are regularly transported to the island from mainland lumberyards, concrete suppliers, and hardware stores, but island building does have a cost premium for such services.

The Brunkers set up their own personal account with the Madeline Island Ferry Lines and had almost daily deliveries of building supplies. They had to get creative more than once to get the job done, often relying on their own sweat equity. As one of the Brunkers told me, "The children would hand a board to mom on the ladder who would pass it to dad on a higher ladder who had the nailing gun."

ABOVE The porch wraps the cool north and east sides of the cabin. Access to the path down to the shore is to the right.

A visitor noted in the cabin guest book, "The design is amazing because it never felt like there were that many people until we all sat down to eat together." One of the keys to packing this amount of space into a compact volume is to expose the ceiling structure on both the main and second levels—it's a great way to add spatial height inside without the cost of taller outside walls. (And if you use fir, pine, or Parallam® structural wood, it can add a lot of character to the rooms.) To reduce the bulk of the volume, the entry facade roof drops low over the wood-storage room.

Les and Theresa note, "We named our home 'Rendezvous' to symbolize the reason for its being. Whether it is brushing teeth in the dormitory-style bathroom next to your brother-in-law or watching the sun disappear over the horizon and resting in the solace of the moment, memories are made in this unique home."

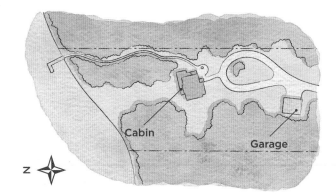

Cabin

Garage

N

The modest cabin character belies the ample living space. The roof drops
low to the left beyond the entry, with an access door for firewood.

As dusk settles over the lake, it's time for hot chocolate and s'mores roasted in the fireplace in this two-family cabin.

FAMILIES RARELY HAVE TIGHTER bonds than those formed by twin sisters, as is the case with Minnesota natives Meghan and Margaret. Their cabin experiences were nurtured on the

Twin-Family Lodge

sleeping porch at their grandma's lake place in central Minnesota. As the twins recall, the large family gatherings over the 4th of July were always hot, tempered only by the welcome porch breezes that allowed them to get some rest. They fondly remember dozing off to the sounds of their parents playing cards and their grandma's snoring in a bed nearby.

When the opportunity arose to create their own shared cabin, Meghan

LEFT The east entry overlooks a grassy sloped play yard. The porch wraps around the northwest corner of the cabin and gives access to the lake.

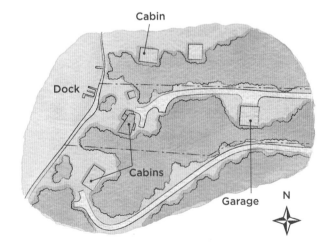

and Margaret knew it would have to be big enough for both families of six, plus grandparents; have a variety of sleeping accommodations as their children grew to adulthood; be open, inviting, and easy to maintain; and yes, have a sleeping porch.

The two couples had selected a lakeside lot with a sunset view in northwest Wisconsin three hours from their city homes. Their husbands, Stuart and Chris, bought the property upon first sight, with only phone calls to Meghan and Margaret to convince them of its charm and potential. The lot had woodland for tree forts, archery practice, and firewood, as well as a shoreline for a boat dock and modest sandy beach. It was well off the busy county highway, quiet and secluded—although their rambunctious gang might well change that.

Architect Dan Wallace and I were charged with the challenge of designing for four decision makers and the inherent conflicts that might suggest. But after a few meetings, it became clear just how close and special the relationships of these families really were.

Sleeping Porches

A screened porch can be an inexpensive means of extending summer living into the fresh air. Used for eating, relaxing, or sleeping, it is a great way to bring in the sounds and smells of nature.

Porch dimensions are the result of an important study of activities, sunlight, and rain intrusion. The length of a porch dictates how many diverse activities it can accommodate, such as dining at a table, lounging on sofa and chairs, or perhaps dozing on a day bed. The width of a porch along with any roof overhang will impact the light available to interior rooms and the distance wind-blown rain will reach the furniture.

Although most screened porches have no additional weather protection, some do have canvas tarps, roll-down vinyl shutters, or quad-hung plastic windows to keep rain, dust, and cool air out.

Margaret notes that their screened porch is the children's favorite place for sleeping. They race to claim beds, and if the beds are full, the floor will have to do. And Meghan adds that they still have some of their grandma's furniture from the old cabin in use on the porch.

Both the screened dining porch and the glazed sleeping porch beyond enjoy lake views.

MAIN LEVEL

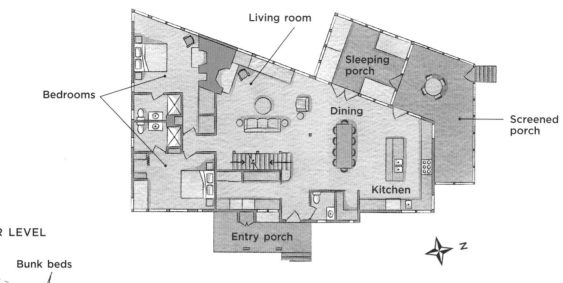

Living room

Sleeping porch

Dining

Bedrooms

Screened porch

Kitchen

Entry porch

N

UPPER LEVEL

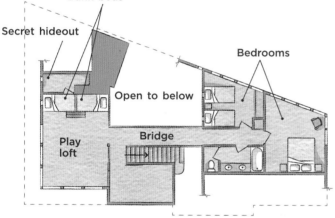

Bunk beds

Secret hideout

Bedrooms

Open to below

Play loft

Bridge

RIGHT The living room is clad in butternut harvested from nearby, and the fireplace is a regional taconite stone. The entire main-level flooring is an easy-to-maintain linoleum.

BOTTOM LEFT A secret child's hideout is reached across one of the bunk beds. Each has a small window for a dapple of natural light.

Dan began the process of setting up an easel out at the site and recording his observations. With stakes locating the setback to the west from the lake, he also noted a side slope difference between a depression to the south and a gentle rise to the north. This change in elevation could allow light into a lower level while still accommodating a main-level entrance from the east near grade.

In previous projects we'd worked on, Dan and I had been exploring the dynamic relationship between trapezoidal floor plans and gable roofs, enjoying the fresh energy created in the form. Deployed here, this relationship created a rising roofline on the lakeside from low at the southwest corner to high at the northwest corner. The higher roof accommodated additional bedrooms with lake views.

On the interior, we created a main level with an open living/dining/kitchen space with easy access to the porch and a modest deck. Two adult suites were added on the quiet south end of the plan, each of a different character. The lakeside bedroom has a fireplace and low, sloping ceiling, whereas the southeast bedroom has a wood-clad arched ceiling.

An open stairway and living room overlook divide the upper level north and south. At the south end, bunk beds slide under the roof. A secret child's cave is accessible between the bunks and is a big hit whenever the children bring friends along. On the north end, two private bedrooms are located with a cascade of windows stepping up concurrent with the rising roofline.

After a few years at the cabin, the families finished off the lower level to address their changing activity needs, creating an additional bedroom, bath, recreation room, and movie room.

Builders Nick Allen and Dave Tworek are craftsmen with access to great local materials. Wormy butternut is their wood of choice for paneling on most of the walls, and recycled Douglas fir is used for the handrails, trim, exposed beams, and handmade doors and cabinets. The fireplace stone is taconite, a byproduct of iron ore mining in northern Minnesota. The flooring on the main level is a durable linoleum, made in part with flax waste from Midwest farms. With a household of wet feet fresh from a sandy beach, it's just the ticket for an easy sweep.

LEFT A bevy of built-in bunk beds is open to the bridge, which overlooks the living space and entry. The ceiling is plywood.

BELOW At the northwest end of the second floor, the roof rises along with cascading windows in a spacious bedroom.

Fun and Functional

The west-side deck with northerly lake view is a favorite spot for dining al fresco or showering off after a morning run. Classic New England cedar shingles and a local flagstone form the palette for this modern cabin.

MEMORIES AND IMPRESSIONS we have as a child vacationing at the same lake summer after summer often inform our decisions later in life for the experiences we seek for own children. The automobile we arrive in and the radio station we listen to may change, but the dive into the water, the s'mores around the bonfire, and the ghost stories told in

Modern Cabin

the dark of night all have a familiar ring to those of the previous generation.

The New York owner of this modern camp had grown up spending summers on the same lake and wanted to extend those experiences to her growing young family of five. When land with a ramshackle fishing shack near her family camp in Vermont became available, she convinced her husband to snap it up. They soon had the shack demolished but not before gaining agreement from the zoning authorities that a new structure could be built of a similar footprint the same close distance to the water.

They hired local Vermont architect Patrick Kane to create a seasonal retreat that would give them ample living space within the limited footprint. The original footprint was a rectangle with the short dimension facing the water, but Patrick was able to get approval for a similar rectangle with the longer dimensions on the lakeside. He created a simple plan of main-floor living with three bedrooms and a bath above. Since extensions for entry and balconies were not allowed, he carved away space from the volume for each. The solid form is clad in the New England vernacular of weathered cedar shingles, yet inside the space and detail are surprisingly modern.

The entry side on the south is close to the road, with windows modest in size except for a high, large trapezoid window that lets light deep into the open stairwell and upper hall. All of the rooms upstairs and down front the water, with expansive north-facing windows that wrap around corners in the living room and kitchen. Guests who walk in for the first time have referred to the windows as a "widescreen lake TV." One

LEFT A covered southwest corner is sheltered from cool northwest breezes.

RIGHT Living/dining/ kitchen share the spectacular panoramic view of the lake through the strategically placed windows. Spruce walls and cabin-grade maple flooring were locally sourced.

ABOVE Entry from the road is to the broad side of the cabin. The large central window floods sunlight deep into the stairwell and living room.

LEFT What looks like a painting on the wall in the bathroom is actually a window, conveniently dropped to bathtub viewing height.

MAIN FLOOR

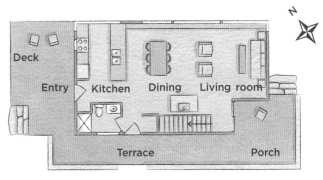

UPPER FLOOR

of the owners' delights is watching storms roll in with their children as the dark clouds form from the north and the wall of rain makes its way across the lake before pummeling against the glass. It's almost as if the camp has just entered a car wash.

While the wide-open main floor is super-conducive to family togetherness, the upstairs is a quiet repose of three private bedrooms. Each bedroom is wrapped in spruce, with ceilings that parallel the roof. The northwest corner bedroom has a small balcony overlooking the water and the westside terrace.

The owners have restructured their professional lives so they can work from the camp in July and August. Spending two months at the camp is just the family bonding experience the mother was hoping for as she extends lakeside pleasures and the memorable lifestyle to yet another generation.

Build Locally

One of the advantages of building in the forested region of northern Vermont is the availability of abundant wood species for harvest and interior use. There are also stone quarries of granite, slate, and soapstone. Patrick Kane takes great pride in supporting the use of local products and in knowing the local craftsmen who are capable of installing them.

Patrick designed many space-saving built-ins for the camp from local pine, including bedsteads, bedside tables, an L-shaped couch, and a coffee table. An old pine tree that needed to come down to make way for the new construction was also milled for use as paneling and furnishings.

The walls and ceilings are sheathed in local spruce, creating the look of old camp rooms. Patrick had decided against using drywall due to the expansion and contraction problems in a building that's left to go cold in the winter. The floorboards are local maple—not the first-grade maple that's used in city homes but rather cabin-grade maple, which has more "character."

The centrally located woodstove sits on a hearth of local Woodbury granite, mined from a newly reopened local quarry. Even the PolyWhey® wood finish, a sustainable alternative to petroleum-based coatings, is from Vermont. (Whey is the residue from milk in the cheesemaking process.)

The northwest corner bedroom has a small balcony lakeside.

An off-the-grid timber-frame cabin is basic shelter at the edge of the wilderness for a family of five. The plan is to install solar panels on the south-facing roof at some point in the future.

THE BOUNDARY WATERS Canoe Area Wilderness (BWCAW) is a million-acre preserve along Minnesota's border with Canada, created in 1978 through an act signed by President

Wee in the Wilderness

Jimmy Carter. Twenty-five years later, it became the getaway destination for Minneapolis couple Steve and Susan. When 20 acres of woods, bogs, and rock outcroppings on the southern border of BWCAW became available (and after an extensive site inspection), they knew it was just the ticket. In the solitude of the forest, eagle shadows wisp by, moose can be seen in the distance, and a wolf's howl pierces the still winter night.

The Big Lift

Eric Mase assembled the cabin's structural roof, roofing material, and gable-end windows on the ground adjacent to where he had assembled the main-floor frame. Working this way, he eliminated the need for scaffolding or ladders. When the roof was complete, he hired a crane for a half day to lift it into place.

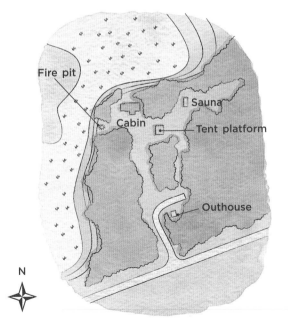

Fire pit
Sauna
Cabin
Tent platform
Outhouse

N

Their early use of the property was for camping, with Steve and Susan first pitching a tent and later building a fixed tent platform. Soon they added an outhouse, and after a heavy spring snowfall capsized a supposedly sturdy tent, a permanent cabin seemed in order. With a modest, off-the-grid structure in mind, they contacted me to guide them into the right course of action.

I visited the site to inspect their preferred building location on top of a 30-ft.-high outcrop with views to the north across the bog. They told me that their needs for shelter for their family of five and occasional visiting friends were modest, as much of their living would be done outdoors. We shared our common appreciation for the book *A Pattern Language* by Christopher Alexander and discussed how many of the 253 building patterns laid forth in that seminal work

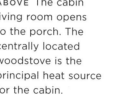

ABOVE The cabin living room opens to the porch. The centrally located woodstove is the principal heat source for the cabin.

BELOW An alternating-tread stair rises to a bridge that connects the gable end sleeping spaces. The stair divides living from dining.

might find applications in their cabin (to name but three: Pattern 117 "Sheltering Roof," Pattern 172 "Garden Growing Wild," and Pattern 236 "Windows Which Open Wide").

I knew that building a small cabin was a challenge—not of design but of finding the right builder who would share the owners' modest vision. In my previous book, *Back to the Cabin*, I had featured work by the WEE CABIN Company, and I thought that builder Eric Mase's unique building system would be most appropriate to the task of creating Steve and Susan's cabin. His timber structure could be precut offsite, under roof and out of the rain and bugs. It could then be assembled onsite with a small crew and a crane (see the sidebar on the facing page). Steve liked the idea of adding his own sweat equity out on the construction site and aiding the erection crew.

ABOVE There is plenty of sleeping space for family and guests in the two lofts connected by the bridge. Cable railings retain the open feeling of the cabin. The timber frame is fir that has been stained, while the floor and ceiling are pine.

LEFT The daytime view from the sink is something the owners never tire of. At night, the northern star is visible.

Eric's building method established a particular modularity that a designer can work within, and he and I soon settled on a three-bay, 14-ft. by 28-ft. frame. To this I added a screened porch and a mudroom. The main floor has porch and living space at the west end, woodstove, kitchen, and stairway in the middle, and dining space on the east end. In the loft space above, there's room for sleeping at each end with a bridge and stairway in between.

The cabin is sited atop the north- and west-facing ledge with open views over the bog below. With the cabin's east/west orientation, one side of the gable roof faces south (ideal for future solar panels), and the porch is warmed by afternoon sunlight. An outhouse, sauna, and tent platform complete the encampment, along with a short driveway off of a forest service road. The whole project is off the grid, with kitchen appliances served by a liquid petroleum (LP) gas tank and heat provided by the woodstove.

Now, after a few years of use, Steve says of his wilderness retreat, "We feel lucky! We found a place in the woods where we can check out (or check in really) with our kids and have a different experience than a weekend at home. And it brings us so much joy that our extended family feels the pull of the place and wants to be there with us. Life is different there; everything takes a little more work, but the simple things seem to have outsized rewards."

A wood-fired sauna known as Wee-Heat provides bathing and a warm respite after a day of cross-country skiing.

MAIN FLOOR

Screened porch

Living

Kitchen

Dining

Mudroom

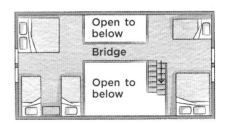

UPPER LEVEL

Open to below

Bridge

Open to below

Add some wheels, crank up the engine, and you
can almost picture this Vermont family cabin
rolling on down to Massachusetts.

THE GREEN MOUNTAINS OF Vermont are an idyllic setting for places of retreat. In northern Vermont, the mountains also provide spectacular sunset views of the Lake Champlain Valley to the

Old Truck Cabin

west. It was just such a setting that encouraged Joan McLane's parents to buy 350 acres of farmland, which was poor in terms of growing potential but had bucolic rolling hills, meadows, forest, and great vistas. It is now the site for Joan and husband Jock's iconic cabin, along with cabins for other siblings, including her brother, Turner Brooks, an architect.

Joan had gone to school in Vermont in her youth and cherished the oppor-

BELOW Old trucks are a family favorite and informed the architect in his design of his sister's cabin.

BOTTOM The living/dining space is a large bay window that expands into the adjoining forest.

tunity to spend summers and short winter breaks in this captivating landscape. As academics in Evanston, Illinois, Joan and Jock's Vermont time was mostly limited to the lush green days of summer. Recently retired, they can now grow a garden and harvest the fall crop in the comforting embrace of a New England autumn. Joan has returned to painting along with reading, walking, and pond swimming in the relaxed life at the cabin.

Turner designed the cabin for the McLanes back in 1976, a time when old metal trucks, trains, and boats found their way into his inventive design process. In the design of the Old Truck Cabin, his fascination with transportation takes the form of a quarter-round roof and twin metal chimneys. Seen from a distance across open meadows, the structure resonates with kinetic energy as if an old abandoned locomotive had come to rest here. To continue the transportation analogy, the third floor resembles a wheelhouse, with a commanding view out over the countryside.

Turner says of his design, "Once in the door of the McLane House, turning left one can pass down a short, low-ceilinged hall to enter the central space of the house that contains living, dining, and kitchen areas. This space that opens outward and

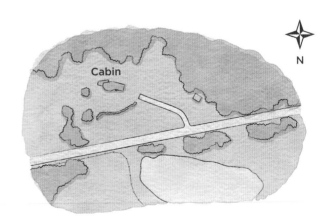

Twin flues
exhaust the
woodstove and
furnace and
rise high in the
two-story living
room next to
a kitchen with
open shelving.
The large interior
window opens to
the second-level
bedroom.

197

Model Cabins

The best way for architects to study cabins with complex roof forms is through three-dimensional models cut from cardboard or balsa wood and assembled with glue. Drawings of floor plans and cross sections are necessary to study precise dimensions, but models tell a holistic tale of form and space.

Architect Turner Brooks made many models that explore the unique shape of his sister's cabin. He also worked as part of the construction crew, appreciating firsthand the complexity of his creation while adding to its detail.

RIGHT A flow of air can be induced by opening interior and exterior bedroom windows along with living room windows below.

upward is like a bay window that has expanded to become the complete living space of the house." Years later, his sister still marvels at the quality of light in this space, where depending on the time of the day, there is always a precious place to curl up with a good book.

The cabin has a bedroom on every level, with baths in proximity on first and second floors. There is a sleeping "cubby" adjacent to the stair on the second floor and plenty of nooks and crannies to snuggle in with a sleeping bag. Joan and Jock prefer the middle-level bedroom, where windows look out across the meadow and an interior window gives overview to the living space below. This window can be opened to allow warm air to float up from the woodstove below, as well as the morning aroma of coffee brewing. The breeze flows freely across their bedroom, and sleep comes easily with the scent of clover and the evening music of the wood thrush.

For 40 years, the McLanes have enjoyed their sojourns in Vermont away from the hustle and bustle of Chicago. In retirement, they even get to spend a few weeks in the cabin in the winter. Of her brother's design, Joan says, "It's simply wonderful."

ABOVE The third floor is a no-frills pine-clad sleeping space, with a view into the treetops.

LEFT A snug sleeping cubby is built in adjacent to the stair. It looks tiny but actually fits an adult (unless he's an NBA star).

FIRST FLOOR

Deck

Dining   Living

Kitchen

Bedroom

SECOND FLOOR

Open to below

Bedroom

Sleeping cubby

Stairs to loft

An abstract composition in twilight attracts this city dweller to her escape in the country. Floor-to-ceiling windows and doors on the back side suffuse the cabin with light.

AN HOUR NORTH UP the Hudson River by train from Manhattan, you arrive in the tranquil village of Garrison, where the stunning river valley is often compared to a Norwegian fjord.

Hudson Valley Retreat

The town is steeped in history and makes a great trailhead for hiking or base camp for visiting American Revolutionary War sites. It was just the sort of tranquility there that attracted a Manhattan professional to build her cabin escape from the hectic life of the city. The short ride from the city made a weekend trip easy and stays of longer duration an enchanting temptation.

The vacationing New Yorker originally enjoyed stays at an older

home along one of the historic supply roads. Rumor of a potential land development across the street encouraged her to purchase this property both for reasons of preservation and environmental concern. Although the home on the site didn't have much pedigree or charm, the red barn and hen house were bucolic, iconic images in an open meadow. After some time and considerable scrutiny, she commissioned architect Sharon Davis to design a modest getaway home on the property. The nondescript house would be torn down and on its exact footprint replaced by an environmentally sensitive, cozy, and modern retreat.

Sharon enjoys puzzles, and her design for the Garrison house reads like a large cube subdivided into eight smaller cubes. Three of the cubes on the back side are carved away to reveal glass walls. This was Sharon's way of making a small structure feel spatially larger. And as a bonus, it creates private outdoor living space on each level so that whether you're inside or out, the focus is on the pastoral view of the meadow.

The five remaining interior cubes comprise 900 sq. ft. and are subdivided into kitchen, dining, and living on the main level and a bedroom and bath above. A floating steel stair and open lightwell connect the levels and add to the feeling of openness.

TOP From the street, the cabin looks like a casual vernacular shed, concealing its distinctly contemporary interior on the glass-filled garden side.

ABOVE The glass wall of the bedroom opens to an east-facing roof deck.

MAIN LEVEL

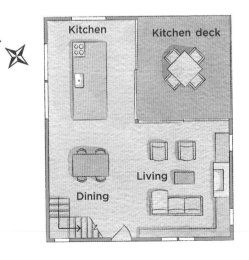

UPPER LEVEL

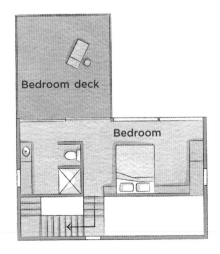

ABOVE A black slate fireplace, black metal stairs, white paint, and reclaimed wood comprise the stark palette of this serene interior.

LEFT Looking for the kitchen? It's nothing more than the concrete island with sink and appliances all to serve the modest dining table.

The one bedroom in the cabin is a spare composition of wardrobe, desk, and bookshelf railing . . . and the bed, of course.

Geothermal Heating and Cooling Systems

Geothermal heating and cooling utilize the constancy of the earth's temperature to dissipate excessive heat or coolness through underground piping. Either vertical wells or horizontal trenches that pipe loops of fluid are induced to flow by an electrically driven pump. The heat or coolness is then transferred across blown air to serve a dwelling.

Geothermal systems perform best in locations where summer cooling needs and winter heating needs are approximately equal. This seasonal balance helps the ground stabilize to the annual average temperature. Geothermal systems are commonly associated with a high cost of installation and low cost of operation.

Fully retractable glass sliding doors to the kitchen deck and bedroom deck enhance the connection to the outdoors.

The house is capped with a shed roof and clad on public sides in weathered gray wood. Only small windows and an unadorned entry door face the neighborhood. To passersby on the historic road, it looks like another vernacular building added to those already in the meadow.

The environmentally sensitive features include recycled pine on the exterior and reclaimed oak inside. A black walnut tree that needed to be taken down was milled and made into furniture designed for the house. Slate clads the fireplace and is also used on countertops and the bathroom wall. Geothermal heating and cooling systems and soy foam exterior wall insulation further reduce the home's environmental impact.

Landscape designer Thomas Woltz added low walls and stairs that connect to the barn and anchor the house to the land. A regional bluestone sheaths the stairs and terraces and was brought indoors in the bathroom. He embellished the site with native plants, including wildflowers seeded in the meadow.

The owner's reverence for nature encouraged her to minimize clutter in the interior space so as not to visually interfere with the panoramic view. "I'm crazy about light; it impacts the way I feel," the owner exclaims. "I love waking up to the view."

RIGHT The living room opens up to the full two-floor space along the stairwell wall.

BELOW Cor-ten® steel adds a warm hue to the planter wall adjacent to the entry stair.

ABOVE The side view of the cabin reveals the contrast between the wooden shed and the glass-and-steel meadow façade.

ORCAS ISLAND IS THE LARGEST of the San Juan Islands in Puget Sound in northwest Washington. It attracts many vacationers who come to enjoy its glorious scenery, old-growth woods, diversity of wildlife . . . and its artistic inhabitants. It is exactly the qualities of place that encouraged Peg O'Hara and Dwight Weber to come back

Color Me Cabin

to Orcas for many years whenever vacations rolled around. They began to dream of a day when they could live on Orcas full time and started the search for an island retreat with charm and great views.

An existing cabin that satisfied their goals never materialized, and although they were loath to take on a new building project, a perfect unbuilt site eventually captured their hearts. It was quiet, secluded, and with an amazing view of Mount Baker on the horizon. And building new allowed them to dream about the perfect plan that would fit their needs to a tee.

Their next step was to find an architect who could both guide them through the design process and oversee

The east-facing, glass-sheathed living room of this colorful family cabin overlooks Puget Sound.

construction when they were back home in Portland, Oregon. They sought advice from area businesses and were happily surprised that the architects recommended were familiar to them by sight at the local grocery store. Susan Stoltz and David Kau were locals and knew well the zoning constraints, building codes, and contracting companies for building on the island. Susan and David asked great questions, and Peg and Dwight's fear of building was soon laid to rest.

Their project evolved to encompass three structures: a primary cabin of 1,400 sq. ft., an artist studio with guest bedroom, and a "curmudgeon hut," where Dwight could sneak away for the best sound system on the island. Peg and Dwight wanted something quirky, comfortable, and eminently livable. As the design progressed, Peg had only one significant critique, "Add more color to the place."

For Peg, color is the antidote to the gray weather of northwestern Washington. She wanted vermilion-colored soffits to

ABOVE No dead space in corner cabinets here as the windows open to the view. Casual open shelving and accessible wine racks make cooking fun and easy.

LEFT Vermilion soffits and forest green siding liven up the adjacent art studio.

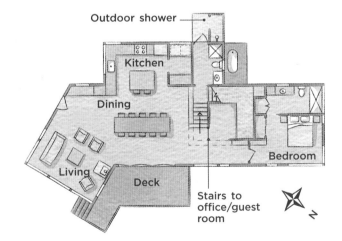

With accordion doors open, the long dining
table extends outdoors onto the deck.

Color

With almost an infinite array to choose from, color is always a great challenge for cabin architecture. Clients or covenants may suggest finding a cabin color in the natural surroundings, but what color is not found in nature? The Minnesota state flower found in cabin country is pink, iridescent moss is lime green, and blueberries are a purplish blue.

Color is a major feature of the work of Stoltz/Kau Architects, and their knowledge of what looks good in the environment of the San Juan Islands is well developed. Together with Peg, they settled on Benjamin Moore® paints:

2002-10	2141-20	HC-10
Vermilion	Cabbage Patch	Stuart Gold

Whatever color you are considering, it's always best to try a sample on the surface material you'll likely use, in the setting where you intend to use it, and at all times of the day. When holding a color swatch in your hand, position it vertically if you're choosing for a wall or turned upside down above your head for the ceiling.

warm the reflected light, gold as a substitute for the sun, and a deep mossy green to emulate the surrounding forest.

Also high on Peg's wish list was a big table for gatherings of friends, family, and the board meetings of the local co-op. Lots of readily accessible bookshelves would be needed for readers of all ages. And an outdoor shower and stock tank bathtub were preferred for bathing al fresco.

The studio had its own requirements, which included garage doors for opening up activities to the outdoors. In addition to their artistic interests, Peg and Dwight imagined rolling open the doors for cocktail gatherings, dancing, and even some karaoke.

Now in retirement, Peg and Dwight have moved to Orcas Island year-round and extend their activities to gardens and orchard planting. They love the way their encampment works for them, supporting the casual life they had always dreamed of.

LEFT A book wall known as "the crate" encases the stairway and the TV room, where built-in seating doubles as guest sleeping.

ABOVE The kitchen cabinets are plywood with a concrete countertop. Clerestory windows drop filtered light into the dining space.

LEFT On the potentially darker, forest side of the cabin, the walls are painted yellow as a substitute for the sun. And there's not only an outdoor shower but also a tub for casual outdoor bathing.

SOUTH DAKOTA IS NOT widely known for its lakes, yet there are several in the state and locals know where to find them. Mark's extended family grew up in northeast South Dakota where

Stargazer

there are a number of prairie lakes, some shallow and popular for duck hunting and others deep enough for swimming, fishing, and recreational boating. Mark occasionally went along with family and friends on trips to this region, and he slowly began to form an attachment to this part of South Dakota. At some point, he began to dream of having a cabin of his own there one day.

Later, married to Jean and with children, Ellen and Paul, Mark

This three-level modern family cabin, banked into the western hill, replaced an old fisherman's cabin on the property.

knew just where to search for recreational property for his family. The prairie lakes of his youth were just two hours from his home and practice. City neighbors invited his family to join them at his favorite lake, and he began to size up his preferred shoreline. When the opportunity to buy a hillside cabin at a central location on one of the best lakes presented itself, he snapped it up. He saw past the old cabin on the property and, together with Jean, imagined the new structure they would someday build for their family.

The lot on the western shore of the lake has a steep drop from a car-access point higher up the hill. Mark remembers well the windy and rainy day they moved into the existing cabin, carrying old junk up into an awaiting dumpster and new belongings down. Mark and Jean appreciated the exercise the 38 steps provided from their many treks with groceries down and garbage up, but they looked forward to extended seasonal use where snow shoveling a stairway wasn't necessary. Friendly neighbors with a new hillside cabin suggested that an architect would be invaluable to come up with a solution for this challenging site.

When they brought me into the design of their new retreat, I immediately envisioned a bridge spanning from the car access to the top of an enclosed stairway. With a two-level drop to the water, we settled on mid-level living in a three-level plan. In this

ABOVE Access from the street is across a bridge into the third level. The cement-board-sided tower at right terminates in a stargazing roof deck.

RIGHT The living room opens onto an expansive deck with a southeast corner view down the lake.

ABOVE Wood kitchen cabinets and island, as well as the flooring, add warmth and contrast to the white walls. The space is compact, so family life can be shared.

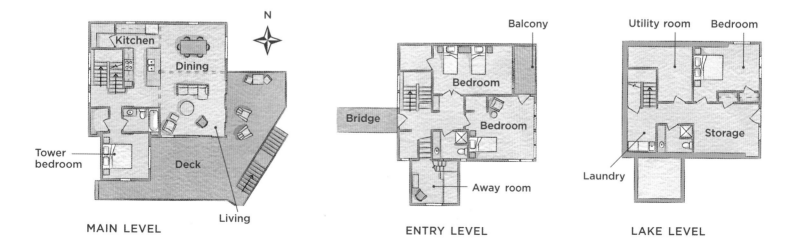

MAIN LEVEL

Kitchen

Dining

Tower bedroom

Deck

Living

N

ENTRY LEVEL

Balcony

Bedroom

Bridge

Bedroom

Away room

LAKE LEVEL

Utility room

Bedroom

Storage

Laundry

ABOVE A small away room on the entry level tucks under the stair that provides access to the stargazing roof deck.

Enter High or Enter Low?

My experience building cabins on vertical lots has uncovered two common site conditions:

- At river and lake lots, you typically arrive high and drop low.

- At ski-in–ski-out lots, on the other hand, you arrive low and lift high.

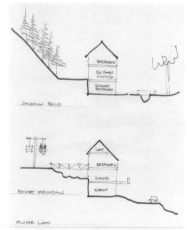

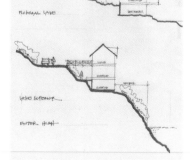

ABOVE A broad deck on the second level overlooks an active beach and boating area. Cable rails meet the safety code while not impeding the downward view.

way, groceries need only be brought down one level from the entry to the kitchen, and later in the day hors d'oeuvres could be carried down just one level to the pontoon boat.

Jean's preference was for a modern structure, with some added features for a fun cabin experience at the lake. Along with my colleague, Paul Buum, we created a stargazing tower that houses the couple's bedroom next to the living space, an away room on the bridge level, and a step stair up to a rooftop perch. The very top of the tower is a private perch for suntanning and the perfect spot to catch a shooting star streaking across the Milky Way.

The entry-bridge level has bedrooms for Ellen and Paul with a shared balcony. Mid-level living is extended outdoors onto a deck with great eastern views over the lake. The lowest level has a guest bedroom along with water-gear storage for a quick exit to the boats.

Mark, Jean, family, and friends are now enjoying their lake experience in all seasons. Fishing, waterskiing, and leisure boating remain favorite summer activities, while cross-country skiing and snowshoeing provide vigorous winter exercise. Mark notes that he always appreciates arriving in winter to a quiet pastoral lake . . . and that the wind has already cleared the snow from the bridge.

Prospects for the Future

What looks like log walls is actually billowy concrete painted yellow. The rounded effect is created by the fabric forms used when the concrete is poured.

"I'LL HUFF AND I'LL PUFF and I'll blow your house in," said the Big Bad Wolf to the Three Little Pigs. The wolf successfully demolished two houses made of straw and sticks, but

Concrete Cabin

finally the house of masonry saved the frightened little pigs.

Designer/builder Sandy Lawton and architect Eleanor D'Aponte didn't need to experiment with houses of straw or sticks but went straight to poured concrete for the first house in the conservation development Sandy had developed in upstate Vermont. A New York City client was looking for a modest cabin with low maintenance and high longevity. Sandy's knowledge of and experimentation with concrete and her proximity to the site made for an easy choice of designer and a great collaboration.

The rural property with steep driveway access was a charming site but not one that was ideal for large trucks carrying precast walls and formwork or for cranes to unload there. It was easier for a concrete-mixer truck to negotiate the slope, so cast-in-place, reinforced, fabric-formed walls became the construction method of choice. Formwork could be built on site, and the end result was interior and exterior walls with a uniquely evocative character.

The cabin design that Eleanor and Sandy came up with is a simple gable vernacular form with a shed roof entryway. The main floor is a central great room with living, dining, and

RIGHT In the open living space downstairs, the concrete walls and floor are complemented by steel structural elements and railings along with wooden beams and ceilings.

BELOW The bucolic Vermont setting for the cabin is at the edge of a wood adjacent to a westerly meadow. The cabin is a blend of traditional cedar shingles and modern concrete and industrial sash windows.

ABOVE/RIGHT The living/dining area opens to an outdoor covered porch on the forested east side, extending the social space of the cabin in fair weather.

kitchen functions and a bedroom and bath. The great room is a high space with a concrete stair leading to a balcony, two sleeping berths, and an additional bath. The room opens to a porch along the east side of the cabin and features a majestic nine-square window on the south side.

The walls of the main body of the cabin are constructed of fabric-formed concrete rising 14 ft. to the roof eaves. By contrast, the gable ends are of standard frame construction, sheathed on the outside in heavy textured shingles. It's a striking contrast in finishes. The one-story entry is sheathed in vertical board and battens.

ABOVE The modest bedroom on the main floor has the feeling of a ship's cabin and is wrapped in cherry wood.

TOP LEFT Two open sleeping alcoves are built into the eaves on the second level.

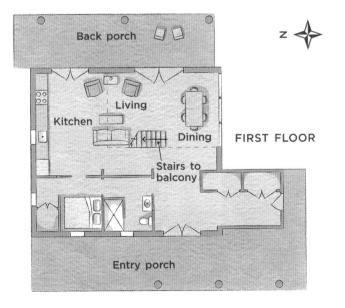

FIRST FLOOR

SECOND FLOOR

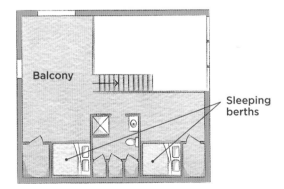

ABOVE A gas fireplace along with in-floor radiant heat warm the interior on cool fall days. The background "pillowed" wall provides a soft counterpoint.

OPPOSITE A poured concrete stair is a significant sculptural element in the living room. The nine-square industrial sash window faces south for passive solar gain.

Wood is used extensively on the interior, and steel also makes its presence known as girder beams, stair, and balcony railings and the large southern window frame. The palette of steel, wood, concrete, and glass fuses together in a contemporary interpretation of a vernacular barn interior.

Sandy refers to the concrete cabin as a wonderful experiment. "It takes a long time to take something from the idea stage through its iterations and to refinement, but this is definitely a step in the right direction." People who have seen the cabin in person have compared the exterior character to a Vermont log cabin. Eleanor says, "We thought the design would be more akin to an agrarian villa. We always wanted something that looked like it could be part of the land. People ride bikes up to the cabin and touch it. We like that."

Concrete Sandwich Wall

The concrete wall system used in the cabin is a sandwich composed of a 4-in. outer layer of concrete, a 3-in. middle panel of polyisocyanurate insulation, and a 5-in. inner layer of concrete. The insulation has fiberglass tie rods that position the insulation in the wall and tie the two outer layers of concrete together. The roof bearing sits on the thicker inner layer of concrete. Electrical outlets and conduit are placed in the inner layer before the concrete pour.

This concrete sandwich wall system is manufactured by Thermomass®. Walls built with this technology can have a variety of textures and shapes depending on the type of formwork used. The exterior concrete is low maintenance, and the interior concrete adds thermal mass to ballast internal temperature swings.

WHEN CABINS GET INTO your blood, there's just no antidote. For the owners of this prefab retreat, the cabin experience was instilled at an early age with each of their families regularly summering at cabins and camps in the eastern United States. Marriage and professional lives brought them to Montana, an epicenter of the great outdoors. Here

Some Assembly Required

they could ski, kayak, mountain bike, trout fish, hike, and camp in all directions just minutes outside the city. Yet the desire to have their own slice of nature with a permanent structure, a cabin, endured.

They hunted for property within a two-hour drive and settled on a remote site just 45 minutes from Yellowstone National Park. From a high altitude, the property overlooks the river valley with views of magnificent mountain peaks to the east. After buying the land, they set about clearing and prepping a site for a cabin. They built a high

Board-and-batten cladding and metal window and door shields protect this modest family cabin in Montana.

MAIN LEVEL

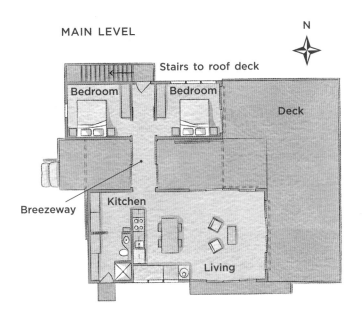

N

Stairs to roof deck

Bedroom

Bedroom

Deck

Breezeway

Kitchen

Living

platform to pitch a tent on, which they hoped would be safely out of reach of the native grizzly bears and mountain lions. By the time they were ready to build, they knew their property well, where the sun rises, where winter winds blow, and what animal paths traverse the site.

The following year, they brought architect Dan Harding out to see the property and he marveled at the spectacular views. When returning later with surveyors, he was also moved by the amount of bear scat on the site. Grizzly bear scat! He knew that he'd need to address security, both when the cabin was vacant but even more so when the couple and their two daughters were in residence.

Dan's design juxtaposes two structures that frame a breathtaking view to the peaks to the east. The living space module to the south has a gable roof reminiscent of the tent platform the family had installed previously. To the north is a modern flat-roof sleeping room module with a secure outdoor stair to its roof deck. The breezeway (or "dogtrot") between the two buildings has two doors that can be operated to secure the structure when no one is present or to create a secure outdoor living area protected from bears. Beyond the two modules, a broad deck faces east.

LEFT No matter the season, the Rocky Mountain view is spectacular.

ABOVE The two components of the cabin are joined by a partially covered outdoor courtyard, which serves as entry and protected exterior living space.

LEFT On the back side, the courtyard can be sealed off for grizzly bear protection at night when in use or when the cabin is vacant.

The Dogtrot

A building form with two enclosed structures on either side of a roofed cover over the open area in between is referred to as a dogtrot. It was a common vernacular form in the southeastern United States during the 19th and early 20th centuries. Such historic structures were made with both log- and frame-building techniques. Dan Harding's southern background and architectural studies at Clemson University made him very familiar with this style.

Mark Twain makes reference to this form (but without naming it) in *Huckleberry Finn:* "It was a double house, and the big open place betwixt them was roofed and floored, and sometimes the table was set there in the middle of the day, and it was a cool, comfortable place."

The kitchen table on wheels doubles as a prep island. The prefab cabinets frame a metal backsplash.

RIGHT The living room opens to the south and east for passive solar gain.

Building on this site was a challenge because the only access was via an old logging trail. Dan and his colleagues set up a prefabrication process that would reduce on-site labor. An on-site concrete mixer truck also seemed unlikely, so they created precast concrete piers. Prefab walls, floors, and roof were fabricated in Helena, Montana.

When all the parts were ready, they were transported to the site in agile smaller trucks and assembled with the aid of a small crane. It took only two days to frame the cabin and then a few more months to finish it off, inside and out. "The snow came in on the first of November, the day we left," says Dan's colleague, Henri Foch. "Our job-site trailer ran off the road coming down the mountain, and we didn't get it out until spring," notes Dan.

The owners enjoy their cabin with family and friends in all seasons. Only the living module contains a woodstove, but with the sleeping loft above it can serve all purposes for a smaller group in winter conditions. In summer weather, the cabin lives large with extension into its secure outdoor world.

RIGHT Sandwiched between the corner of the kitchen and the firewood storage bin, a built-in bench is a great spot to warm your toes while cozying up for an afternoon read.

BELOW LEFT Sleeping on the bear-protected roof deck is a favorite way to end the day for adventurous family members.

This off-the-grid Ohio family cabin perches atop a pristine, sheltered rise overlooking a well-stocked pond on this reclaimed former mining property.

BELMONT COUNTY, OHIO, takes its name from the French word for "beautiful mountain." It is what early settlers likely reflected upon as they opened the land for agriculture and looked

A Cabin Off the Grid

across meadows at the western side of the Appalachian Mountains. It is the beauty of what John Dutton knew in his youth before open-pit mining in the 1970s reshaped that view. While he recognizes that mining contributed to his welfare, he is particularly pleased that reclamation has now brought beauty back to the scene. Ohio environmental laws of the time required coal companies to install ponds and plant trees and native grasses.

TOP The surrounding property is pastureland for the family's cattle farm.

ABOVE From the outside, the rectangular cabin looks like a utilitarian shed with a rusty red roof.

On the cattle farm that he and his wife, Rita, own in Belmont County, there is a reclamation site that captured his imagination. The former pit is now a 16-acre lake stocked with fish, and the once-scarred landscape has new foliage, wildlife, and clear sky above.

Their son Greg had recently completed an architectural degree, and after a few years of apprenticeship with area firms he was looking for a project of his own. He took it upon himself to design a cabin for the reclamation site and presented the design to his dad on Father's Day 2012, with a commitment to see it built. Greg was encouraged by the building site his parents had selected, a place he'd frequented often as a teenager, riding horses or ATVs and sneaking the occasional beer.

Greg envisioned the cabin as a simple, long vernacular shed, with two bedrooms at the east end, a modest living and kitchen space in the middle, and an open porch with a fireplace where the family could enjoy sunset views to the west. The cabin is built with a basic palette of materials: cedar siding and Cor-ten metal roof on the outside and drywall and polished concrete floors on the inside.

In the environmental spirit of the reclamation, it is purposely off-grid and low maintenance. Power is supplied by a solar cell array 50 yards from the cabin, and energy is stored in a battery bank located in an adjacent shed. During the overcast days of winter, the system is backed up by a propane-fired generator. The south-facing windows allow an intimacy with

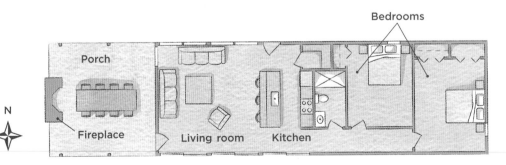

Bedrooms

Porch

Fireplace

Living room

Kitchen

N

ABOVE The kitchen island also serves as breakfast counter or buffet entertainment when dining moves to the porch.

LEFT The south-facing glass adds to passive solar heating, warming the concrete floor inside.

ABOVE A bank of sliding-glass doors opens the cabin to a terrace with views over the man-made lake.

nature and also play a role in the passive solar design. Heated by the sun, the concrete floors return the heat to the space when temperatures cool. A natural spring on the property contributes water that is stored in a cistern.

The cabin was completed in July in preparation for Greg's wedding at the site in August. But they would need one additional structure: a pavilion to shelter their guests. Although his fiancée, Liz, knew of the project, she wasn't aware of the scope, scale, and ultimately delightful character of the pavilion. The wedding was planned for the first weekend in August, and Liz had left for work in California in May and wasn't returning home until a couple of days before the event. Construction of the pavilion didn't start until less than two weeks before the wedding. In Greg's words, "I think getting it completed was the only part of the wedding I was nervous about. We were working on it up until the big day and getting finished just under the wire."

The cabin and the pavilion have now become a popular location for events for family and friends, with Rita taking on the role of chief scheduler. John has extensive plans for relocating an old barn to the property to use as event space, and they are developing trails, docks, and a walkway bridge. The family is grateful to be able to share the beauty of their land with others and to honor the history of farming, mining, and social gathering of this region.

In Greg's words, "This beautiful piece of ground that was enjoyed passively by few is now a hub of gathering my family and our friends. It is where we have weddings, reunions, birthday parties, and fun fall nights by the fire. In the morning, you look out of the living room's floor-to-ceiling windows to see the fog lifting off the lake, a school of geese making their way across the water, and a herd of cattle grazing in the pasture. It's incredible!"

BELOW A pavilion on the property makes an ideal spot for events for family or friends, from weddings to banjo-picking concerts.

In this distinctly modern interpretation of the cabin, roof planes tie in with the horizon and vertical lines mirror the tree trunks. Glass planes define social spaces, while the opaque planes obscure private realms.

THE INTIMATE, COZY CABINS of the past are opening up dramatically to become glass and steel environments that blur the boundaries of inside and out. This is particularly true in the

Inside Out

Pacific Northwest and in the benign climatic conditions of Puget Sound. Easily accessible from the metropolises of Seattle, Tacoma, Vancouver, and Portland, the Sound is an excellent location for getting away from a hectic urban life. Lush pine forests, seaside views, and sparse development enhance its bucolic charm and the demand for glassy open architecture.

Harry and Claudia Bray were drawn to the area from Portland, Oregon, three hours away. They purchased

ABOVE Inside or out? It's tough to tell at first glance, but this is the magnificent view from inside the living room across Puget Sound to the Olympia Mountains beyond.

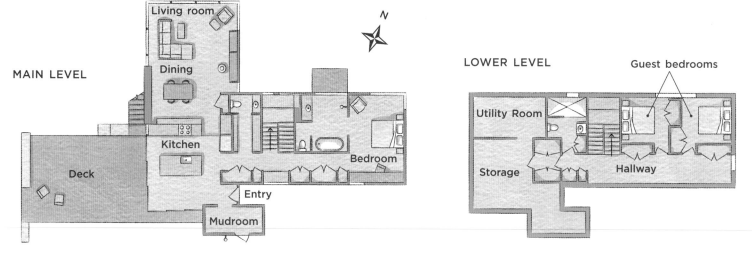

MAIN LEVEL

Living room

Dining

Kitchen

Deck

Entry

Mudroom

Bedroom

N

LOWER LEVEL

Guest bedrooms

Utility Room

Storage

Hallway

20 acres on the Key Peninsula, where the charm factor was the light filtering through the trees and the water view to the Olympic Mountains in the distance. Not so charming was the cramped little red cabin on the property, drafty with a slight list and housing several families of mice. The Brays and their two grown children made do with this humble abode for three years. Then, with a total change in mind, they hired MW Works, a Seattle architectural firm, to create their radically new mode of retreat.

"I wanted an indoor/outdoor quality that makes the best of the northwest climate," notes Harry. They also wanted an interior that was "rustic and not too precious," explains MW architect Eric Walter. He and partner Steve Mongillo created a modern, Bauhaus-style ensemble of glass, steel, and wood. The design ensures that the owners remain connected to nature at all times.

The plan accommodates primary living on the main level and guest sleeping on a lower level, which is exposed by the hillside site. According to Harry, "When it's the two of us, we just use the upper level and there's no sense of emptiness. Or there can be six of us here and it doesn't feel like too many people." The design created 1,400 sq. ft. on the main level and another 800 sq. ft. on the lower level.

ABOVE Walnut cabinets display family artifacts and a dry supply of firewood for the stove.

LEFT The living/dining/kitchen space opens at either end into nature, the whole composition unified by a pine ceiling and polished concrete floor.

Northwest Modern

Northwest Modern is a regional style of architecture developed in the Pacific Northwest in the middle of the 20th century. It is a blend of vernacular local materials and the International style, initiated in the Bauhaus in Germany in the early 20th century. The Bauhaus promoted clean lines, an absence of ornamentation, and an emphasis on industrialization. The past two decades have seen a rebirth and flourishing of Northwest Modern in homes and cabins in Washington, Oregon, and British Columbia.

The style is characterized by extensive use of glass, unpainted wood, steel, asymmetrical floor plans, and flat or low-pitched roofs. Cabin design remains a rich testing ground for Northwest Modern, continuing to explore the intersections between built form and nature.

ABOVE An expansive ground-level deck lies just off the kitchen. The most dramatic view awaits those who ascend the open stair to the roof deck.

RIGHT Indoor and outdoor cooking are intertwined: The concrete countertop inside morphs into a concrete island outside.

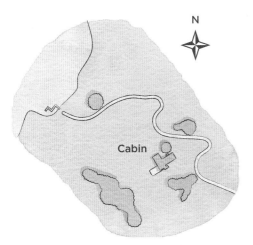

RIGHT Tight-knot cedar paneling sets off the white plumbing fixtures in the couple's bathroom.

BELOW Glass corners even in the bedroom reinforce the interconnectedness of sheltered space and nature.

The design process created solid blocks of more private spaces and an open pavilion of social space exposed to the view. The expanses of glass are the defining feature of the exterior, punctuated by walls sheathed in cedar. The same cedar is brought indoors in the kitchen, hallway, and couple's bathroom. The ipé (Brazilian walnut) deck flooring also transcends inside and outside.

In contrast to the light-toned natural cedar, a dark walnut is used for the cabinets and casework, which blends with the black window frames. Pine plywood sheathes the ceilings, with its light hue reflecting sunlight deep into the interior spaces. A few walls are painted a medium gray as a background to all the warm wood.

The Brays cherish their indoor/outdoor cabin and have made the most of their environs for a variety of activities. The water encourages kayaking, beachcombing, and some oyster farming. The forest is for hiking, western tanager spotting, and foraging for mushrooms. And in the winter rainy season, they enjoy reading, listening to great music, and staring at the rain.

"This place is so serene, it makes me suspend all my worries," chimes Claudia. "When we leave, we feel fortified." It is exactly what the Brays wanted as a contrast to their 1920 foursquare in Portland. "Friends tease us for calling our modern structure a cabin," notes Claudia, "but that's just what it is . . . a little cabin in the woods."

The entry side of this West Virginia prefab cabin is deceptively narrow, belying the amply gracious, two-level interior within.

PREMANUFACTURED CABINS CONSTRUCTED

in a factory and transported to the site have been available for nearly a century in the form of what is commonly known as "mobile homes."

Transported to Nature

They began as caravans and were truly mobile but soon became parked in stationary positions in mobile home parks or remote country sites.

Several attempts have been made over the years to take the caravan look out of the module and reformulate the character to look like a home, cottage, or cabin. Many of us have passed a half of the "double-wide" home rolling down a freeway but rarely take notice of the home or cabin once it is set.

ABOVE The galley kitchen serves both interior and exterior dining in a getaway where cooking is clearly high on the owners' agenda.

MAIN LEVEL

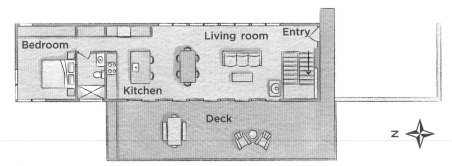

In January 2003, *Dwell* magazine sponsored a competition for a well-built modern-looking prefab home. Three winners were selected: Modern Modular by Resolution: 4 Architecture on the East Coast; the FlatPak house by designer Charlie Lazor in the Midwest; and the Glidehouse by Michelle Kaufmann Designs on the West Coast. With considerable fanfare, the first home was constructed in 2004 in Chapel Hill, North Carolina, with Resolution 4 partner Joseph Tanney in charge. Other modular home companies across the United States capitalized on this competition to serve a new and growing clientele. The WEE HOUSE Company (featured on pp. 188–193) presented its first product as a retreat cabin.

By 2008, Tanney had several Modern Modulars built or underway when Chris and his wife, Sarah, approached him to design a modern getaway from their home in Washington, D.C. They had specifically selected a hillside in West Virginia because it was within a two-hour drive and had liberal zoning laws and relaxed building inspection requirements regarding modular homes. As Chris puts it, "The approval process was a breeze. I paid $250, got a building permit, the end."

The initial plan was for a simple 16-ft. x 64-ft. box, but Chris and Sarah worried that it might be too claustrophobic. A walkthrough of a similar structure that Resolution 4 was building on Long Island reassured them that it would be comfortable. "And the truth is, if our cabin were any wider, you would lose the way things come through it—the light, the wind, and

TOP The bedroom on the main floor catches a corner southwest view into the forest.

ABOVE The lower level has two guest bedrooms as well as additional living space for movie watching or relaxing.

LOWER LEVEL

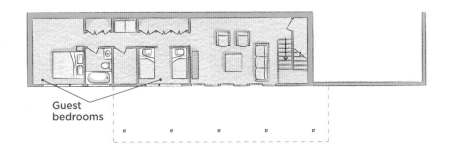

Guest bedrooms

ABOVE The main level living room is just inside the entry and convenient to the lower-level stair. A Scandinavian woodstove adds warmth and complements the modern appearance.

RIGHT A generous south-facing deck doubles the living space of the cabin.

the feeling that you are up in the trees." Adding a walkout basement under the prefab box allowed them to double the size of the cabin for just 50 percent more money.

The long, linear plan has a solid uphill side and a glass-filled downhill viewing side. Entry to the cabin is through the living room, with the wet areas of the kitchen and bathroom in the middle and the couple's bedroom at the far end. A stair located near the entry makes it convenient for carrying guest luggage to lower-level bedrooms.

The building process in the factory went smoothly, as did the highway drive to the site. The challenge was the steep drive up onto the hill, especially at a switchback turn. A bulldozer was necessary to expedite the final ascent. The module was set on a basement foundation after which a deck was added. A woman drove by during the process and stopped to stare. "What's that?" she asked. "Some kind of double-wide trailer?" Chris just smiled and said, "Yes, it's a double-wide."

After seven years of delightful use and rental, Chris and Sarah have passed the property along to Sharon Baker. "Living in the city is great, but being able to get away, conveniently and completely, is a privilege," she says of her new retreat. "I'm not much of a 'roughing-it type of person,' so it was important to me that the cabin be a place that transported me out of the city but wasn't without the comforts of home."

Sharon enjoys the whole process of going to the cabin, from packing up the family and the two dogs to making the two-hour drive. Cabin anticipation lightens the conversation and gives time to prep the grocery list for the small-town market along the way. Cooking for friends and family at the cabin is special for Sharon, and her guest book is already filling with stories of proposals, anniversaries, birthdays, and surprise getaways. She reveals, "It sounds a bit hokey, but the biggest thing I have gotten out of this little cabin in the woods is a sense of connectedness. Not just to the beauty of West Virginia but to others with whom we share our lives.

ABOVE From the deck, the view is out over the West Virginia hills aglow in the sunset.

The Varieties of Modular Experience

Modular construction can be created in a wide variety of floor plans and stacked in numerous ways.

It's hard to imagine the dark and dreary cabin that was transformed into this spacious, light- and color-filled Appalachian retreat.

CABINS ARE SOMETIMES A dream waiting to be dreamt. For Linda Perlstein, the dream began in 2002 at a writer's retreat in Wyoming, where she was ensconced in a cabin by a creek to

A Cabin Transformation

write a book. The gurgling water, the slamming of the screen door, and the occasional rustle of the leaves reminded her of those carefree days of her youth at summer camp. She vowed that when back home in Washington, D.C., she would start a search for an Appalachian Mountain cabin. All she wanted was a little hideaway where she could write and think in solitude.

By 2003, flush with a little extra money from her book, Linda began

Butterfly Roofs

A butterfly roof is an inverted gable with one central valley and high eaves at the sides. It is said to have been invented in 1930 by the architect Le Corbusier for an unbuilt project in Chile. The form became quite popular in mid-century modern American homes, with whole subdivisions employing butterfly roofs.

Today, butterfly roofs are notable for collecting rainwater and for accommodating high windows on each of the opposite ends of the building, flooding a space with light. They are usually created with a gentle "cricket" (a raised portion) in the middle of the valley so that water is diverted to each end of the valley, where it can be collected in rain barrels.

ABOVE LEFT Although much of the transformation occurs inside, the ranch-style exterior was modernized with a palette of cement board painted night blue, galvanized ribbed metal panels, and white trim.

ABOVE RIGHT The butterfly roof collects rainwater and accents the roof rise with views into the treetops.

investigating the real estate ads in her local newspaper. Week after week, she perused the ads in search of a property she could afford within a comfortable driving distance for weekend use. She eventually built up the courage to go see a 12-year-old cabin in a lightly populated area just east of the West Virginia state line. It was love at first sight; she bought it!

By the time she closed on the property and began to move in, another love had entered her life: a man called John. When the two of them arrived, they discovered that the previous owners had just walked out the door and left everything behind—beds, books, games, and dishes. As Linda reveals, "We cleaned house and sold much of it at the local firemen's support sale. I priced it all cheaply so it would sell, but what I really wanted was to meet all my country neighbors."

The cabin had been built as an unheated seasonal structure, and it took some time to open and close it each time they visited, especially in the winter. After a few years, John, now her husband, got tired of all the surprises that greeted them upon entry. A burst pipe, a family of bats, or a decomposing rodent in a trap was not a great start to a relaxing weekend getaway.

Linda and John quickly grew to love the setting of their mountain getaway and the small-town life nearby. With a first child on the way, they realized they'd need another sleeping space, a better kitchen, and possibly a rejiggering of the plan

LEFT The screened porch is a welcome extension of the living space at this mountain hideaway.

BEFORE PLAN

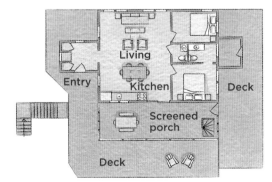

Entry

Living

Kitchen

Deck

Screened porch

Deck

AFTER PLAN

N

Kitchen

Bedrooms

Living room

Rolling barn door

Guest bedroom/ writer's studio

Deck

Screened porch

ABOVE Transom windows high in the new ceiling bring filtered light deep into the living room. Manufactured roof trusses are exposed and painted white to reflect light.

RIGHT The rolling blackboard panel can be moved to shut off the office/guest bedroom from the living space.

so they could better appreciate the view. But most of all, Linda wanted a soaking bathtub and a place to write.

Local architects Beth Reader and Chuck Swartz have an imaginative spirit and are known for their familiarity with modest budgets and local builders, so they were a logical choice for the cabin upgrade. "We had a choice between the architect who designed Jiffy Lubes®, or the one who drew inspiration from a Jiffy Lube garage door in the design of a home," says Linda. "We easily chose the latter."

Beth and Chuck helped them visualize the proposed transformation, whereby a significant L-shaped addition as well as some judicious remodeling would result in an open, airy plan. They flipped the kitchen to the back side of the cabin and slid the porch to the corner to open up the living area to the view. They also flipped the roof from a standard gable to a butterfly style to flood the living space with light. They added a room that doubles as a guest bedroom and writer's studio, with large rolling barn doors to open the space to the living area. They reorganized the plan so that all the plumbing was over a heated crawlspace in the addition, and they gave Linda a view from her bathtub.

Beth and Chuck were a spirited duo to work with, and they channeled their energy into creating the cabin that Linda had always dreamt of, complete with the sounds of nature nearby and the familiar, reassuring slam of that old screen door. As Linda has it, "Now we always arrive with a smile on our faces and joy in our hearts."

ABOVE/RIGHT The use of bold color is a recurring theme throughout the cabin, from the wainscot in the bathroom to the walls and carpeting in the child's bedroom.

A cabin in a remote mountain meadow opens to panoramic views in northeastern Washington.

JESSE, SUSAN, AND THEIR son, Theodore, escape their Vancouver home for the six-hour trek to northeastern Washington State as often as possible. They enjoy the vast landscape,

Cabin in the Sky

irregular rock outcroppings, sagebrush, pine trees, and many lakes—quite a contrast to the damp, gray urban life of Vancouver. They typically stay for longer periods in the summer months but try to get there once a month for weekends year-round and always for the annual celebration with friends at Thanksgiving. Winter may present challenges for access, but the solitude

Prospect and Refuge

Much like our animal ancestors, human beings like to seek a place of refuge in a well-protected enclosure from which they can look out over the surrounding terrain. Prospect and refuge theory has been connected to the work of Frank Lloyd Wright, and his designs have a very open social side (prospect) and relatively solid sleeping side (refuge).

The search for prospect leads us to cabin sites with a view, at a precipice, or at the water's edge. We look for places where we might enjoy nature through exploratory forays out from our protected base.

Refuge may be found by nestling up to a hillside, a forest, or the solidity of an enclosure of our own creation. Within a structure there can be degrees of refuge, with sleeping spaces typically seeking the greatest level of safety. Even the location of a bed is often thought best on the wall opposite the bedroom door.

ABOVE The inverted roof sheds water to a collection point for future harvesting, while a solar array (at left) energizes the cabin. An outdoor patio extends the living area.

RIGHT Coats and hats on hooks define a minimalist mudroom at the front door.

and vast whiteness are intensely stimulating and well worth the journey to this remote location.

In architectural terms, *prospect* is the search for overlook, which Jesse and Susan desired strongly and were able to achieve by building in an open, arid site, devoid of tall vegetation, with exceptional views to the Cascade Mountains to the south. Just below the cabin, they catch glimpses of farmers' fields, and they are just a short drive away from vineyards, orchards, and farmers' markets.

The metallic box they built on a plateau just below a foothill is a *refuge* in this potentially hostile environment. The isolation of the site necessitated an off-grid solar installation for electrical generation and the use of propane for water heating and cooking. The principal heat source is a modest woodstove. The remote site also promoted a construction method where on-site labor would be minimized.

The exterior walls and roof panels are built with cross-laminated timber, which consists of three, five, or seven layers of dimensional lumber, layered perpendicular to one another and glued together to provide dimensional stability, strength, and rigidity. Because of the remote location, the panels were prefabricated at a panel facility 50 miles away, transported to the site, and erected in a couple of days. The roof panels, only 4 in. thick, span the 24-ft.-square envelope and have a unique

LEFT Whether eating inside or out, the view to the Cascade Mountains is spectacular.

BELOW The only openings on the sheltered western side are the two bathroom windows stacked in the corner of the cabin. The exterior is rusted steel.

ABOVE The desk in the upper-level bedroom overlooks the dining room below. The walls are whitewashed pine.

RIGHT Susan and Jesse enjoy cooking together in their galley kitchen. The openings in the wood-clad wall above are to the hall and bedroom.

FIRST FLOOR

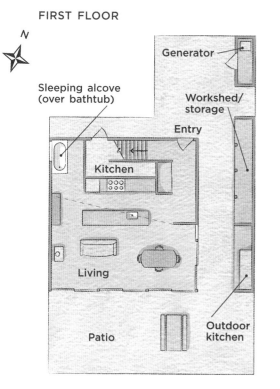

SECOND FLOOR

ABOVE LEFT/ RIGHT A one-of-a-kind sleeping alcove in the western corner of the main floor has a bed that can be raised, revealing a bathtub below!

fold that provides structural rigidity to the volume and aids in shedding snow loads.

The exterior is sheathed in plate steel panels, sized to an 80-lb. maximum so Jesse and his brother could lift them into place during the build. The 2-ft. x 10-ft. panels are secured to the wood walls with fasteners that accommodate the diurnal and seasonal dimensional movement of steel. The steel is left to weather into a rusty hue, looking a lot like the old abandoned mining structures found in nearby hills.

The interior stud walls were built on site and contain all the plumbing and electrical systems. These walls are sheathed in pine to match the cross-laminated timber. All of the pine walls were then whitewashed, a technique Jesse had seen when working in Norway.

The 24-ft.-square plan has two levels, with entry, living, dining, and kitchen on the main floor, as well as a unique guest-sleeping alcove overlaying a bathtub (see the photos above). The second level contains a bathroom, clothes closet, and a bedroom that overlooks the living space below. Even though it's only 850 sq. ft., the cabin has a surprisingly spacious feel. "Much more so than our city apartment of the same size," notes Susan.

CREDITS

Front matter photographers:
p. (i–iii) Susan Teare; p. (iv) Carolyn Bates;
p. (v) Troy Thies; p. (vi) Troy Thies; p. 1 Troy
Thies (top), Carolyn Bates (left), Susan Teare
(center right), Eric Morley (bottom right);
p. 2 Troy Thies; p. 4 Susan Teare; p. 5 Shai
Gil; pp. 6–7 Susan Teare

All drawings by Christine Erikson, except as
noted below.

HISTORY LESSONS

Opener (PP. 8–9)
PHOTO: Susan Teare

A CABIN WITH A HISTORY (PP. 10–17)
PHOTOS: Susan Teare
BUILDER: Elk Mountain Contracting;
www.elkmountaincontracting.com

THE CAMP THAT KEEPS ON GROWING
(PP. 18–25)
PHOTOS: Troy Thies

PEACE CABIN (PP. 26–31)
PHOTOS: Susan Teare
LOG CABIN SPECIALIST: John Ming
GENERAL CONTRACTOR: Larry Pilkenton

WELCOMING CABIN (PP. 32–37)
PHOTOS: Troy Thies
ARCHITECT: Dale Mulfinger, FAIA, SALA
Architects

WINDSWEPT (PP. 38–45)
PHOTOS: Susan Teare
ARCHITECT: Robert Knight, Knight
Architect, www.knightarchitect.com

ALL ABOUT THE PORCH (PP. 46–51)
PHOTOS: Troy Thies
ARCHITECT: Dale Mulfinger, FAIA, SALA
Architects

FOR EVERYONE A VIEW

Opener (PP. 52–53)
PHOTO: Troy Thies

FAMILY MEMORIES (PP. 54–61)
PHOTOS: Susan Teare
DESIGNER: Milford Cushman with Kelley
Osgood, Cushman Design Group,
www.cushmandesign.com
BUILDER: Donald P. Blake, Jr.

HEAVENLY HAVEN (PP. 62–69)
PHOTOS: Rob Karosis
ARCHITECT: Rob Whitten, AIA, Whitten
Architects, www.whittenarchitects.com

TRUSTWORTHY (PP. 70–75)
PHOTOS: Troy Thies
BUILDER: Hod Ludlow

IN SEARCH OF A MOUNTAIN CABIN
(PP. 76–81)
PHOTOS: Todd Crawford
ARCHITECT: Duncan McPherson, AIA, Sam-
sel Architects, www.samselarchitects.com

IN THE TREETOPS (PP. 82–87)
PHOTOS: Susan Teare
DESIGNER: Tory Wolcott

MOTHER'S PLACE (PP. 88–95)
PHOTOS: Troy Thies
ARCHITECT: Dale Mulfinger, FAIA,
SALA Architects
BUILDER: Roland Kristofferson

NATURE'S BOUNTY

Opener (PP. 96–97)
PHOTO: Shai Gil

ISLAND CABIN ON ELBOW LAKE
(PP. 98–103)
PHOTOS: Troy Thies

HIGH COUNTRY TIMBER FRAME
(PP. 104–109)
PHOTO: Shai Gil
ARCHITECTURAL DESIGNER: Peter Moffet

TROUT FISHING IN MINNESOTA
(PP. 110–115)
PHOTOS: Troy Thies
ARCHITECT: Dale Mulfinger, FAIA, SALA
Architects

ESCAPE TO BOONE MOUNTAIN
(PP. 116–121)
PHOTOS: Eric Morley
ARCHITECT: Thomas Barrie
Architect, AIA, www.thomasbarriearchitect
.com

STEALTH CABIN (PP. 122–127)
PHOTO: Shai Gil
ARCHITECTS: Andre D'Elia and
Meg Graham, superkül, www.superkul.ca

A MAINE ISLAND CAMP
(PP. 128–135)
PHOTOS: Jeff Roberts
DRAWINGS (P. 131): Melissa Andrews
ARCHITECT: Will Winkelman, AIA,
Winkelman Architecture, www.winkarch
.com

NESTLED TOGETHER

Opener (PP. 136–137)
PHOTO: Bill Sallans

FISH CREEK CABINS (PP. 138–145)
PHOTOS: Susan Teare
ARCHITECT: Shawn Ankeny, AIA, Ankeny
Architecture and Design,
www.ankenyarchitecture.com

THE LUXURY OF PLACE (PP. 146–151)
PHOTOS: Susan Teare
ARCHITECT: Sarah Nettleton, FAIA (guest
cabin and shed)

SHARED COMPOUND (PP. 152–157)
PHOTOS: Bill Sallans
ARCHITECT: Matt Garcia, Matt Garcia
Design, www.mattgarciadesign.com

TREE HOUSE (PP. 158–163)
PHOTOS: Chris Ermides, *Fine Homebuilding*
ARCHITECT: Michael McDonough,
www.mcdonougharchitect.com

FULL HOUSE (PP. 164–171)
PHOTOS: Troy Thies
ARCHITECT: Dale Mulfinger, FAIA, SALA
Architects

TWIN-FAMILY LODGE (PP. 172–179)
PHOTOS: Don Wong
ARCHITECTS: Dale Mulfinger, FAIA, and
Dan Wallace AIA, SALA Architects

FUN AND FUNCTIONAL

Opener (PP. 180–181)
PHOTO: Carolyn Bates

MODERN CABIN (PP. 182–187)
PHOTOS: Carolyn Bates
ARCHITECT: Patrick Kane, Kane Architecture, www.kanearchitecture.com

WEE IN THE WILDERNESS
(PP. 188–193)
PHOTOS: Troy Thies (except p. 193:
Dayna Mase)
ARCHITECT: Dale Mulfinger, FAIA,
SALA Architects
BUILDER: Eric and Dayna Mase

OLD TRUCK CABIN (PP. 194–199)
PHOTOS: Susan Teare (except p. 198, left:
Turner Brooks)
ARCHITECT: Turner Brooks, Turner Brooks
Architect, www.turnerbrooksarchitect.com

HUDSON VALLEY RETREAT
(PP. 200–205)
PHOTOS: ©Elizabeth Felicella/Esto
ARCHITECT: Sharon Davis Design,
www.sharondavisdesign.com

COLOR ME CABIN (PP. 206–211)
PHOTOS: Andrew Buchanan (except p. 210:
courtesy Benjamin Moore)
ARCHITECTS: Susan Stoltz and David Kau,
Stoltz Kau Architects, www.stoltzkau.com

STARGAZER (PP. 212–217)
PHOTO: Troy Thies
ARCHITECTS: Dale Mulfinger, FAIA, and
Paul Buum, AIA, SALA Architects
BUILDER: Wes Holmquist

PROSPECTS FOR THE FUTURE

Opener (PP. 218–219)
PHOTO: Jeremy Bittermann

CONCRETE CABIN
(PP. 220–227)
PHOTOS: Carolyn Bates
DESIGNER/BUILDER: Sandy Lawton,
Arro Design, www.arrodesign.org
ARCHITECT: Eleanor D'Aponte, AIA,
Studio Neva

SOME ASSEMBLY REQUIRED
(PP. 228–233)
PHOTOS: Derik Olsen
ARCHITECT: Dan Harding, Intrinsik Architecture, www.intrinsikarchitecture.com

A CABIN OFF THE GRID
(PP. 234–239)
PHOTOS: Carolyn Bates
ARCHITECT: Greg Dutton, Midland Architecture, www.midlandarch.com

INSIDE OUT (PP. 240–245)
PHOTOS: Jeremy Bittermann
ARCHITECTS: Eric Walter and Steve Mongillo, AIA, MW Works Architecture+Design,
www.mwworks.com

TRANSPORTED TO NATURE
(PP. 246–251)
PHOTOS: Susan Teare (except p. 251,
bottom: courtesy Joseph Tanney, Resolution:
4 Architecture)
ARCHITECT: Joseph Tanney, Resolution:
4 Architecture, www.re4a.com

A CABIN TRANSFORMATION
(PP. 252–257)
PHOTOS: Susan Teare
ARCHITECTS: Beth Reader, FAIA, and
Charles Swartz, FAIA, Reader & Swartz
Architects, www.readerswartz.com

CABIN IN THE SKY
(PP. 258–263)
PHOTOS: The Morrisons
ARCHITECT: Jesse Garlick, Platform
Architecture + Design, www.p4ma.com

If you like this book, you'll love *Fine Homebuilding*.

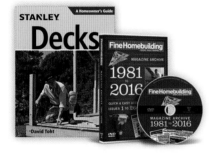